Saipan, Guam, and Peleliu, 1944

US Marine

VERSUS

Japanese Soldier

COMBAT

Gregg Adams

Illustrated by Johnny Shumate

OSPREY PUBLISHING
Bloomsbury Publishing Plc
Kemp House, Chawley Park, Cumnor Hill, Oxford OX2 9PH, UK
29 Earlsfort Terrace, Dublin 2, Ireland
1385 Broadway, 5th Floor, New York, NY 10018, USA
E-mail: info@ospreypublishing.com
www.ospreypublishing.com

OSPREY is a trademark of Osprey Publishing Ltd

First published in Great Britain in 2024

A catalog record for this book is available from the British Library.

ISBN: PB 9781472861139; eBook 9781472861146;
ePDF 9781472861153; XML 9781472861160

24 25 26 27 28   10 9 8 7 6 5 4 3 2 1

Maps by www.bounford.com
Index by Rob Munro
Typeset by PDQ Digital Media Solutions, Bungay, UK
Printed and bound in India by Replika Press Private Ltd.

Osprey Publishing supports the Woodland Trust, the UK's leading
woodland conservation charity.

To find out more about our authors and books visit
www.ospreypublishing.com. Here you will find extracts, author
interviews, details of forthcoming events and the option to sign up for
our newsletter.

Acknowledgments

Research for this book was aided by the US Marine Corps' History
Division, US Navy History and Heritage Command, US Army
Combined Arms Research Library, and the US Army Center for Military
History, which have digitally scanned thousands of historic original
documents and photographs and have made these available to the
public via the internet. The author especially acknowledges Ms Nancy
Whitfield, Archivist, Historical Resources Branch, Marine Corps History
Division, for providing copies of scanned USMC reports used in research
for this book. Additionally, the author thanks Mark Stille for providing
copies of relevant volumes from the postwar Japanese Monographs series.

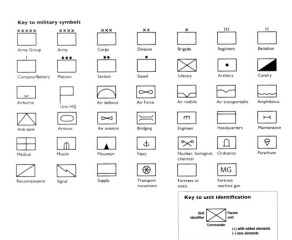

CONTENTS

Introduction

On February 24, 1944, the last Japanese defenses on Eniwetok Atoll, in the Marshall Islands, were reduced. The atoll was quickly developed into a US forward naval base. The United States now had a base 2,000 miles from Tokyo and less than 1,200 miles from the Mariana Islands. Unlike small atolls captured thus far in the Central Pacific, however, the larger islands of the Marianas archipelago had sufficient ground area to allow for the construction of large airfields for US Army Air Forces (USAAF) Boeing B-29 Superfortress long-range heavy bombers. From airfields in the Marianas the B-29s could bomb Japan, with Tokyo less than 1,500nmi away. The need for airfields from which B-29s could launch their raids on Japan and a desire to liberate Guam, a prewar US territory, made the Marianas the next objective for US forces under the command of

These Japanese troops were part of the invasion force – 500 men of the IJN's 5th Base Force and the 5,500-man IJA South Seas Detachment (144th Infantry Regiment, reinforced) – that captured Guam on December 10, 1941. US forces stationed on Guam consisted of 271 US Navy personnel including five nurses, 153 US Marine Corps personnel, and a poorly trained indigenous Insular Defense force of 246 men. Japanese officials renamed the island "Omiya Jima" (Great Shrine Island) and ordered that all schools teach Japanese. (Hulton Archive/ Getty Images)

The senior American commanders for the Marianas operation. From left to right: Vice Admiral Richmond K. Turner, USN (commander, Joint Attack Force); Lieutenant General Holland M. Smith, USMC (commander, Expeditionary Troops); Admiral Raymond A. Spruance, USN (commander, Fifth Fleet); Vice Admiral Marc A. Mitscher, USN (commander, Fast Carriers); Major General Roy S. Geiger, USMC (commander, IIIAC); Rear Admiral Richard L. Conolly, USN (commander, Southern Attack Force); and Brigadier General Pedro A. del Valle, USMC (artillery commander, IIIAC). (USN 80-G-235994)

Admiral Chester W. Nimitz. Planning began for the capture of Guam, Saipan, and Tinian, the latter two of which were prewar Japanese territories.

Seizing the Marianas would not be easy, however, as Japan considered the islands critical to the defense of the Home Islands. Frantic efforts were made by the Japanese to reinforce the islands' defenses. The Imperial Japanese Army (IJA) sent two divisions and three large expeditionary forces organized from detachments from other divisions to the Marianas. Once on the islands and before any US attack, the three expeditionary forces were reorganized into two independent mixed brigades (IMBs) and two independent mixed regiments (IMRs). The Imperial Japanese Navy (IJN) spent the first half of 1944 preparing for the long-desired decisive battle against the US Navy; and given the Marianas' location, a US invasion would provide the catalyst for this major fleet battle. The IJN's Combined Fleet reorganized most of its force into the First Air Fleet centered on its three fleet carriers and six light fleet carriers with 473 aircraft. Carrier aircrew attrition since the start of the Pacific War had been heavy; as a result the aircrews of the First Air Fleet had less than six months' training.

The US forces attacking the Marianas, designated Fifth Fleet, were significantly more numerous, technologically superior, and better trained than their Japanese counterparts. The three principal components were: the Fast Carrier Task Force, Task Force 58 (TF 58); the amphibious force (TF 51); and the landing forces (TF 56). TF 58 included seven fleet carriers (CVs), eight light fleet carriers (CVLs), and 956 carrier aircraft. US Navy carrier aircrew had two years' training and 350 hours' flight time before being sent to sea. By mid-1944 almost all US Navy carrier pilots were combat veterans. TF 56 was composed of two amphibious corps (IIIAC and VAC). Within these corps were three Marine divisions (2d, 3d, and 4th), one Marine brigade (1st Provisional), and one US Army infantry division (27th). A second US Army division (77th) was brought forward in July for use on Guam.

MAP KEY

1 February 23: Eniwetok Atoll in the Marshall Islands – soon to serve as a US forward naval base supporting the capture of Saipan, Guam, and Tinian in the Mariana Islands – is captured by US forces. On June 1, 1944, Eniwetok Atoll was the most westward US base in the Central Pacific.

2 March–June 1944: While the Americans prepare to attack the Mariana Islands, the Japanese heavily reinforce the Caroline Islands, including their major naval base at Truk Atoll. The US advance to Saipan, Guam, and Tinian, and then to Peleliu Island in the Palau Islands, leaves over 100,000 Japanese sailors and soldiers isolated on bypassed Central Pacific islands.

3 June 15: VAC lands two Marine divisions on Saipan. The island is secured by July 9 after VAC is reinforced by one US Army infantry division.

4 July 21: IIIAC lands on Guam with one Marine division and one provisional Marine brigade. One US Army division is landed as reinforcements and Guam is secured on August 10.

5 July 24–August 1: VAC seizes Tinian through a shore-to-shore amphibious attack from Saipan.

6 September 15: The 1st Marine Division lands on Peleliu. The island is secured on November 27, 1944, after the US Army's 81st Infantry Division relieves the battered Marine division.

7 September 23: US troops secure the undefended Ulithi Atoll in the Carolines. The atoll is quickly developed into one of the largest forward fleet operating bases for US forces.

8 October 17: Sixth US Army lands on the island of Leyte in the Central Philippines.

9 November 24: The 73d Bombardment Wing USAAF bombs Tokyo for the first time from Saipan with 111 B-29 Superfortress long-range heavy bombers.

US amphibious doctrine had been continually refined since the 1942 landing on Guadalcanal in the Solomon Islands. Until the Marianas operation, landings had been made on larger South Pacific islands or small atolls in the Central Pacific. At Guadalcanal, New Georgia, Bougainville, and Cape Gloucester on New Britain, invasion beaches had been either lightly defended or undefended. Other than Tarawa Atoll in the Gilbert Islands, the small Central Pacific atolls attacked had limited Japanese defenses. In the Marianas, however, volcanic islands would be invaded across defended beaches with Japanese artillery deployed to shell landing sites. Fortifications were built on and behind the beaches, and reserves were positioned for counterattacks. In accordance with their established doctrine, the Japanese would strive to defeat the US landing at the water's edge. If this failed, they would counterattack the beachhead and drive the enemy into the water.

The US invasion of Saipan on June 15, 1944, triggered the joint IJN and IJA *A-Go* plan, which called for Saipan's garrison to crush VAC forces on the beaches while the First Air Fleet defeated the US fleet. The two fleets fought the largest battle between aircraft carriers, the Battle of the Philippine Sea, on June 19–20, 1944. The IJN lost about 500 aircraft, two fleet carriers (*Taihō* and *Shōkaku*) sunk by submarines USS *Albacore* (SS-218) and USS *Cavalla* (SS-244) respectively, and one light fleet carrier (*Hiyō*) sunk by TF 58 aircraft. The US Navy lost no ships and only 130 aircraft. The IJN's carrier force was shattered for the rest of the Pacific War. On Saipan, the Japanese failed to stop the Marines on the beaches and were reduced to isolated bands. Saipan was declared secure on July 9, 1944.

Guam was invaded by IIIAC on July 21, 1944. As planned, the island's IJA garrison attempted to stop the US landing at the water's edge. When this

Once ashore and moving inland, Marines frequently had to advance through rugged terrain. Here, members of a rifle squad move among trees and through the remains of a shattered structure in an area that has been subjected to naval shelling. These Marines are stripped for battle; they have left their packs and other items behind and are carrying ammunition, water, first-aid kits, and emergency rations along with their weapons. (Keystone/Hulton Archive/ Getty Images)

failed, a major Japanese counterattack was launched against the 3d Marine Division during the night of July 25/26. This action was defeated with heavy losses to the IJA units. The survivors fought on until Guam was declared secure on August 10, 1944.

Defeats suffered by the Japanese at sea and on land in the Marianas campaign led to a re-evaluation of island-defense doctrine. The Japanese high command recognized that because the IJN could not defeat the US Navy, island garrisons were becoming isolated outposts. Orders were issued to island garrisons to conserve strength, prolong their defense, and inflict as many US casualties as possible.

This new Japanese doctrine was encountered by the 1st Marine Division on Peleliu Island in the Palau Islands. On Peleliu a fiercely contested landing on September 15, 1944, was soon followed by a struggle for the rugged coral ridges. Having sustained heavy losses, the 1st Marine Division was replaced by the US Army's 81st Infantry Division on October 20. Peleliu was not secured until November 27, 1944.

This work examines the contest between US Marines and IJA troops in three actions. The first action examines the Japanese effort to stop the 4th Marine Division landing on Saipan at the beach through the use of artillery and fixed beach defenses. The second action examines the IJA's July 25–26 counterattacks on Guam that attempted to crush the 3d Marine Division's beachhead four days after the US landing. The third and final action examines the assault by troops of the 1st Marine Division on Peleliu against the IJA's 2d Infantry Regiment during the first days of a prolonged battle of attrition.

The Opposing Sides

ORGANIZATION AND EQUIPMENT

US Marine Corps

In 1944 US Marines were volunteers who had either enlisted directly in the US Marine Corps, or draftees who had volunteered for the US Marine Corps during induction. This resulted in Marine riflemen being of higher quality than riflemen in most US Army infantry divisions. US Army infantry (other than the Airborne and Rangers) was filled with the draftees left over after the USAAF and other technical branches had made their selections. Considering themselves "volunteers" gave Marines (and US Army Airborne troops) a high *esprit de corps* which resulted in higher standards of aggressiveness, initiative, and unit cohesion. Comparing themselves to some of the US Army infantry divisions they fought alongside in the Pacific fostered the Marines' belief that they were an elite force.

The US Marine Corps had been growing since the start of the Pacific War. By June 1944 there were two Marine amphibious corps headquarters (IIIAC and VAC), five divisions (1st–5th), one provisional brigade (1st) with two regiments (the 4th and 22d Marines), various supporting ground units, and a large aviation component. With both IIIAC and VAC assigned to the Fifth Fleet in the Marianas, a temporary command, Fleet Expeditionary Troops, was established to oversee the corps. Major General Holland M. Smith USMC was given this command while retaining command of VAC. On July 12, 1944, Smith, now a lieutenant general, assumed command of the newly established Fleet Marine Force Pacific (FMFPac), which took administrative charge of all US Marine Corps ground and air forces in the Pacific. FMFPac was a subordinate command of the US Pacific Fleet. Smith was replaced at VAC by Major General Harry Schmidt. IIIAC was led by Marine aviator Major General Roy S. Geiger.

VAC had yet to command in a land battle. Its previous operations in the Gilbert and Marshall islands had seen individual division- or brigade-size landings on small coral atolls. IIIAC, originally designated the I Marine Amphibious Corps, had commanded both the 3d Marine Division and the US Army's 37th Infantry Division on Bougainville, which gave the commander and staff of IIIAC greater experience controlling a multidivision force on land. On Saipan, VAC commanded three divisions (two US Marine Corps and one US Army) and on Guam IIIAC commanded one Marine division, one Marine provisional brigade, and one US Army division.

Marine divisions in the Marianas and on Peleliu were organized under the US Marine Corps' Series F Table of Organization (T/O), officially issued on May 5, 1944; but before that date, units started to reorganize using drafts of the new T/O released in January 1944 and the Series F infantry regiment T/O issued in March 1944. In February 1944 the 2d and 4th Marine divisions started their restructuring, which was completed in May and April respectively. The 1st and 3d Marine divisions reorganized during May and June. The two infantry regiments of the 1st Marine Provisional Brigade were organized as Series F regiments during the same period.

The Series F T/O streamlined the Marine division by reassigning several units as corps-level assets and eliminating others. A Marine division now had 843 US Marine Corps officers, 119 US Navy officers, 15,548 enlisted Marines, and 955 enlisted sailors. In contrast, the previous Series E divisional T/O was composed of 908 US Marine Corps officers, 133 US Navy officers, 17,236 enlisted Marines, and 1,688 sailors. The Series F division consisted of three infantry regiments (each with 3,218 all ranks), one artillery regiment (2,639), one M4A2-equipped tank battalion (630), one engineer battalion (904), one pioneer battalion (745), one service battalion (751), one motor transport battalion (539), one medical battalion (599, mostly US Navy personnel), one headquarters battalion (1,004), and a divisional headquarters (257). Each division had 10,953 .30-caliber M1 Carbines, 5,436 .30-caliber M1 Garand semiautomatic rifles, 853 .30-caliber M1918A2 Browning Automatic Rifles, 302 .30-caliber M1919A4 light machine guns (LMGs), 162 .30-caliber M1917A1 medium machine guns (MMGs), 161 .50-caliber

US small arms. The top weapon is an M1 Carbine, the middle is an M1 Garand rifle cut down to the length of an M1 Carbine, and the bottom is a regular M1 Garand. A Series F Marine division, with 16,503 men, carried 5,436 M1 Garands and 10,953 M1 Carbines into action. Artillerymen, engineers, pioneers, supply troops, service units, and administrative personnel were armed with M1 Carbines. (Archive Photos/Getty Images)

M2 heavy machine guns (HMGs), 36 37mm M3A1 towed antitank guns, 12 75mm M3 halftrack self-propelled mounts (SPMs), 24 75mm and 24 105mm howitzers, 117 60mm M2 mortars, 36 81mm M1 mortars, and 46 M4A2 medium tanks. Amphibian tractor (amtrac) battalions were reassigned as corps-level assets and special-weapons battalions and engineer regimental headquarters were eliminated.

Series F infantry regiments consisted of a Headquarters and Service (H&S) company (261 all ranks), one weapons company (203), and three infantry battalions (918 each). Infantry battalions had an H&S company (213) and three rifle companies (235 each). Rifle-company weapons platoons and battalion weapons companies were eliminated in the Series F T/O. Now a battalion H&S company contained an 81mm mortar platoon and a rifle-company headquarters included a 60mm mortar section. The now-defunct weapons companies' machine-gun platoons replaced rifle companies' weapons platoons. Regimental weapons companies included one platoon of four 75mm M3 halftrack SPMs, and three platoons each with four 37mm M3A1 towed antitank guns.

Series F divisional artillery regiments fielded four battalions, each having three firing batteries. Two battalions were equipped with 105mm M2A1 howitzers and two with 75mm M1A1 pack howitzers. Each firing battery had four guns, giving a regiment 24 105mm and 24 75mm howitzers. The previous Series E regiment had five battalions (three 75mm and two 105mm); the third 75mm battalion was detached and converted into a corps-level 155mm howitzer battalion. This led to the renumbering of battalions within the artillery regiment; the 1st and 2d battalions were equipped with 75mm pack howitzers and the 3d and 4th battalions were equipped with 105mm howitzers.

Marine tank battalions under Series F included one H&S company (123 all ranks) and three tank companies (169 each). The Series E scout company was reassigned to the division headquarters battalion. A tank company had four platoons, each with three 75mm-armed M4A2 medium tanks, and a headquarters platoon with three M4A2s and one M32B2 tank retriever (derived from the M4A2 chassis). In the Marianas campaign the 2d and 4th Marine divisions' tank battalions fielded a provisional fourth company

The M1918A2 Browning Automatic Rifle, or BAR. The Series F Marine infantry T/O allocated three BARs to each 13-man rifle squad. This meant each rifle company had 27 BARs. Although the BAR had a slower rate of fire than the IJA's LMGs, they outnumbered the Japanese infantry's automatic weapons. A Marine rifle squad had more firepower and greater combat strength than an IJA squad. (Military Images/ Alamy Stock Photo)

This Marine NCO, the leader of a rifle squad, is a veteran of fighting in the Northern Solomon Islands in late 1943. Having deployed his squad and issued orders to them, he is firing his M1 Carbine on advancing Japanese infantry. His opponents are from the IJA's III/18th Infantry, which was counterattacking with the intent of driving the Marines back into the sea.

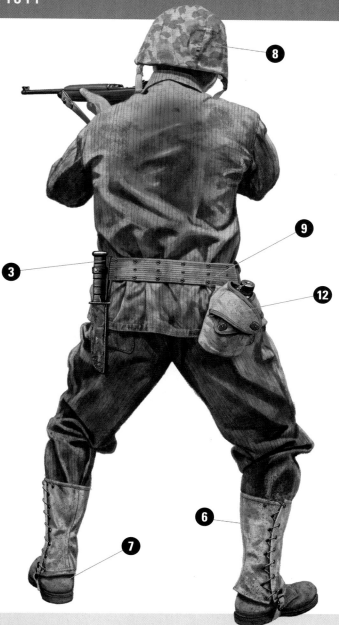

Weapons, dress, and equipment

Firing .30-caliber rounds from a 15-round magazine, the M1 Carbine (**1**) was 35.6in long overall, had a barrel length of 17.75in, and with its sling weighed 5.8lb loaded. A carbine magazine pouch (**2**) that could hold two magazines is attached to the stock. The M1 Carbine did not have a bayonet; instead the user was issued a US Marine Corps Mk 2 combat knife (**3**), weighing 0.7lb and with a 7in blade.

He wears the two-piece HBT uniform, made of heavy, sage-green, herringbone twill cotton. Secured by four metal buttons, the jacket (**4**) had three flapless pockets: one on the left side of the chest, and two on the front of the hips. The trousers (**5**) had a button fly and four pockets. He also wears leggings (**6**) and brown service shoes (**7**). His helmet (**8**) is the M1 model with an optional camouflage helmet cover, which many Marines did not use during the initial landing on Guam.

Once ashore, Marines dropped their packs and any other equipment they considered unnecessary to carry when fighting in the tropical heat. This Marine has an M1936 pistol belt (**9**) with two M1 Carbine magazine pouches (**10**), each carrying two magazines. He also carries an M1924 first-aid pouch (**11**) and a canteen (**12**).

equipped with 18 M3A1 flamethrower-equipped light tanks and six 37mm-armed M5A1 light tanks.

Divisional engineer regiments, which had commanded divisional engineer and pioneer battalions along with a Naval Construction Battalion (NCB, colloquially known as "Seabees"), were eliminated under Series F. The US Navy argued that permanently attaching an NCB resulted in it being wasted between amphibious operations when it could be gainfully employed elsewhere. In the Marianas, the 2d, 3d, and 4th Marine divisions retained their engineer regiments (each with its own NCB) because they had been included in early planning. By the fall of 1944, however, these regiments were disbanded and the NCBs returned to US Navy control. The Series F divisional engineer battalion consisted of a headquarters company (307 all ranks) and three engineer companies (199 each), each with three engineer platoons. A pioneer battalion had a headquarters (127 all ranks) and three pioneer companies (206 each). While pioneer battalions were part of the beachhead logistics system, all pioneers were Marines and had been trained for combat. Pioneers were expected to defend against Japanese attacks and were frequently used in front lines.

The two Marine infantry regiments of the 1st Marine Provisional Brigade were structured using the Series F "separate infantry regiment (reinforced)" T/O. This unit consisted of a Series F infantry regiment as above with a number of company- and platoon-sized combat and support units assigned to it. Combat units included one 75mm pack howitzer battalion, one engineer company, one pioneer company, one tank company, and one reconnaissance platoon. The separate infantry regiment was analogous to a regimental combat team (RCT).

Now non-divisional assets, the 1st–4th Amphibian Tractor battalions were assigned at first to either IIIAC or VAC in May 1944. In September all US Marine Corps amtrac battalions, of which there were now ten, were assigned to FMFPac. Battalions were allocated to corps and divisions as needed for operations. A divisional assault landing required more Landing Vehicles Tracked (LVTs) than were to be found in a divisional battalion of three companies and 486 men. Battalions were sometimes increased to five

A US Marine Corps machine-gun squad with an M1917A1 water-cooled MMG is deployed in support of riflemen advancing in the distance. Marine rifle companies had a platoon with six LMGs or MMGs and used them as needed, although once ashore the Marines preferred to use the MMG. (USMC/Interim Archives/ Getty Images)

companies. An amtrac company had a headquarters equipped with three amtracs and three platoons each with nine amtracs.

Armored amphibian battalions had not been organic to divisions. These battalions were equipped with armored, armed LVT(A)s (A for "Armored"); in summer 1944 these consisted of a mix of 37mm M6 gun-armed LVT(A)-1s and 75mm M2 howitzer-armed LVT(A)-4s. The LVT(A)-4 replaced all remaining LVT(A)-1s after the Peleliu campaign. Armored amphibian battalions (852 all ranks) had an H&S company and four combat companies, each with three platoons of six vehicles each. Armored amphibians were attached to assault regiments and battalions by platoons and companies to provide support to landings. On August 31 the Marines had three armored amphibian battalions, with additional units provided by the US Army.

Corps-level Marine artillery consisted of separate 155mm howitzer battalions (each 650 all ranks) and 155mm gun battalions (738 each). Each separate battalion had an H&S battery and three firing batteries. Each howitzer battery had four 155mm M1A1 towed howitzers and each gun battery had four 155mm M1A1 towed long guns known as "Long Toms." There were six 155mm howitzer battalions; four were formed from battalions made surplus as a result of the reorganization of divisional artillery. Six 155mm gun battalions were organized from the seacoast defense batteries of Marine defense battalions; the defense battalions themselves were reorganized as antiaircraft artillery (AAA) battalions. Eventually, IIIAC and VAC were each assigned three 155mm howitzer and three 155mm gun battalions as corps artillery. Some AAA battalions were assigned to IIIAC and VAC during operations while others provided defense to bases.

Marine regiments were numbered in sequence from the 1st through 29th. All regiments were called "Marine" whether they were infantry, artillery, or engineer. There were 18 Marine infantry regiments, numbered 1st–9th and 21st–29th. Six Marine artillery regiments were numbered 10th–15th. In 1944 the 1st Marine Division consisted of the 1st, 5th, 7th (all infantry), and 11th (artillery) Marines; the 2d Marine Division had the 2d, 6th, 8th (all infantry), and 10th (artillery) Marines; the 3d Marine Division had the

3d, 9th, 21st (all infantry), and 12th (artillery) Marines; and the 4th Marine Division fielded the 23d, 24th, 25th (all infantry), and 14th (artillery) Marines. The 1st Marine Provisional Brigade had the 4th and 22d Marine separate regiments.

Within infantry regiments the rifle companies were designated by letters. The 1st Battalion's rifle companies were A, B, and C; the 2d Battalion's were E, F, and G; and the 3d Battalion's were I, K, and L. Before their elimination under the Series F T/O, the three battalions' weapons companies had been designated D, H, and M respectively, but these were now no longer used. The letter "J" was never used to designate a company, reportedly to avoid confusion with "I" in written orders, reports, and messages. Divisional battalions were numbered with the parent division's number, e.g., 1st Tank, 1st Engineer, and 1st Pioneer battalions in the 1st Marine Division. Non-divisional battalions were individually numbered.

Imperial Japanese Army

On December 7, 1941, the IJA was composed of 51 infantry divisions and 59 separate brigade-sized units. Throughout the Pacific War new units were activated, many with new divisional, brigade, regimental, or battalion T/O structures. Most of these new formations were infantry. In all, Japan raised an additional 172 infantry divisions between January 1942 and August 1945, 35 of which fought in the Pacific campaigns, including two in the Marianas and one at Peleliu.

In spring 1944, Saipan, Guam, and Peleliu fell under command of the IJA's 31st Army, activated on February 18, 1944, and led by Lieutenant General Obata Hideyoshi, to defend the Central Pacific islands. Obata's army assumed command of four existing sector groups: Ogasawara (or Bonin), Marianas, Truk (covering the Carolines), and the Palaus. The Marianas Sector Group was soon split into the Northern Marianas and Southern Marianas groups. In June 1944 the 31st Army's headquarters was located on Saipan.

Pictured in April 1941, this smartly turned-out young Japanese soldier stationed in China carries a bugle on his backpack. When units moved from China and Manchuria to the Pacific they found an enemy who was better trained, organized, equipped, and commanded than the ones they had faced. IJA infantry continued to use bugles in the Pacific, mainly for signaling infantry to attack. In contrast, the Americans increasingly relied on the latest communications technology that soon included hand-held voice radios. (ullstein bild/ullstein bild via Getty Images)

The body of a young Japanese soldier, killed by US artillery fire, remains frozen in a sitting position in the spot where he died on Saipan. His dress and personal equipment are typical of those worn by the Japanese island garrisons. (© Hulton-Deutsch Collection/CORBIS/Corbis via Getty Images)

The IJA used several types of infantry division during World War II, but only one type – the "ocean" (or "sea mobile") division – was encountered on Saipan (43d), Guam (29th), and Peleliu (14th). The 14th Division had been raised in 1904 during the Russo-Japanese War and the 29th Division was formed in April 1941. Both were conventional triangular divisions before conversion to ocean divisions. The 43d Division was established in April 1943 using the existing 63d Independent Infantry Group as its core.

Organized beginning in late 1943, ocean divisions were designed to be transported over coastal waters and between islands by self-propelled barges and consequently had almost no land transport. The barges were not comparable to US assault landing craft, however. Once ashore, ocean divisions relied on manpower for battlefield mobility and resupply.

The ocean division had three infantry regiments that had the division's artillery, engineer, and other units attached to them, giving the division three self-contained combat teams. US intelligence sometimes referred to these as "regimental combat team divisions." On paper, each ocean division was to have an attached sea-transport engineer regiment with approximately 150 self-propelled barges to provide waterborne mobility, but only the 14th Division had its sea-transport regiment. The 14th and 29th divisions were each organized into two island-defense regiments and one sea-mobile (or amphibious) regiment. The 14th Division had the 2d (island defense), 15th (amphibious), and 59th (island defense) infantry regiments, while the

Warrant officer, III/18th Infantry

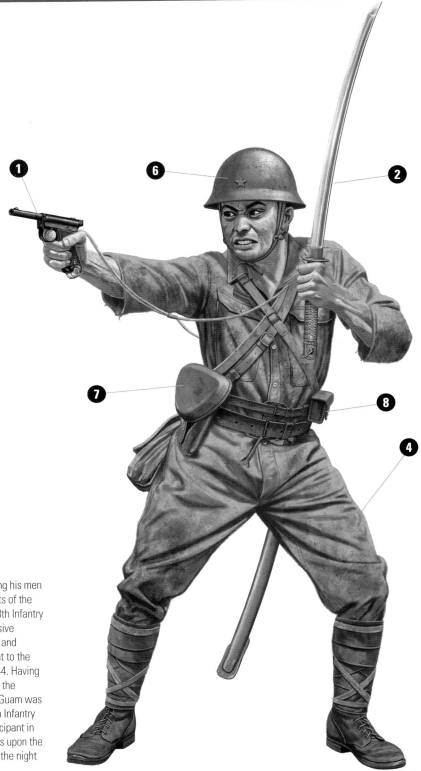

This warrant officer is leading his men in an attack against elements of the 3/21st Marines. The IJA's 18th Infantry Regiment had gained extensive combat experience in China and Manchuria before being sent to the Mariana Islands in April 1944. Having suffered heavy losses when the transport ship carrying it to Guam was torpedoed, the reduced 18th Infantry Regiment was a major participant in the Japanese counterattacks upon the Marines' beachhead during the night of July 25/26.

Guam, July 26, 1944

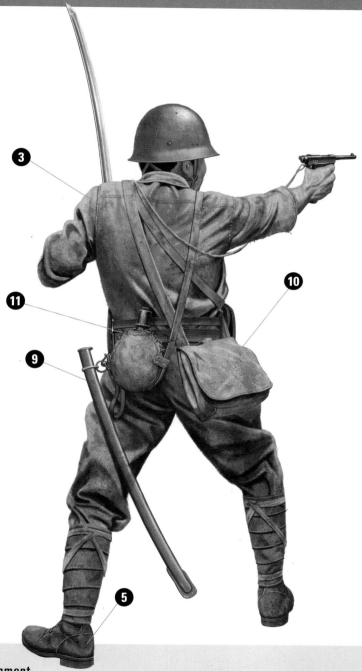

Weapons, dress, and equipment

This warrant officer is armed with an 8mm Type 14 pistol (**1**) and Type 95 sword (**2**).

He wears a summer (tropical) cotton uniform. The shirt (**3**) features an open collar, breast pockets, and three-quarter sleeves, with rank insignia above the right breast pocket. The trousers (**4**) could be full length (as here) or three-quarter length, or loose-fitting breeches. He also wears Type 5 marching shoes (**5**) made of horsehide and

hobnailed with a metal-rimmed heel. His helmet (**6**) is a Type 92, which was of low grade and offered little protection from bullets or shell fragments.

He wears two waist belts, one with the pistol holster (**7**) and cartridge box (**8**) and the other with his sword scabbard (**9**) attached. He has a haversack (**10**) over his left shoulder and a Type 94 canteen (**11**) suspended from a web sling.

29th Division consisted of the 18th, 38th (both island defense), and 50th (amphibious) infantry regiments. Both divisions each contained a divisional tank company with four platoons of four tanks each plus one headquarters tank. The authorized strength (without the sea-transport regiment) of these two divisions was roughly 12,051 men. The 43d Division was different; its three infantry regiments (118th, 135th, and 136th) were island-defense regiments, giving the division a strength on paper of 11,262 men.

Island-defense regiments each had 3,165 men in three infantry battalions, one artillery battalion, one engineer company, one supply company, and one medical unit. Each infantry battalion had three rifle companies and an infantry-gun company. Each such regiment was notionally armed with 1,312 7.7mm Type 99 rifles, 108 50mm Type 89 grenade dischargers, 108 7.7mm Type 99 LMGs, 18 7.7mm Type 92 HMGs, 12 75mm field or mountain guns, six 37mm Type 94 antitank guns, and six 70mm Type 92 infantry howitzers.

Sea-mobile, or amphibious, regiments each had 3,964 men and were transportable by barges. Each regiment contained an engineer company, a light-tank company, a machine-cannon company (20mm automatic cannons), and three infantry battalions. Amphibious infantry battalions each had three rifle companies, one 81mm mortar company, one artillery company (37mm antitank and 75mm mountain guns), and one pioneer platoon equipped as an assault-engineer unit. The sea-mobile regiment's weapons were 1,813 Type 99 rifles, 108 Type 89 grenade dischargers, 108 Type 99 LMGs, 18 Type 92 HMGs, nine 75mm Type 41 mountain guns, 36 81mm Type 97 mortars, nine 20mm Type 97 antitank rifles, six 37mm Type 94 antitank guns, six 20mm Type 98 automatic cannons, and nine light tanks (usually the Type 95 Ha-Gō with a 37mm main gun).

In early 1944, newly organized expeditionary units (EUs) were culled from several divisions of the Kwantung Army stationed in Manchuria and North China to reinforce the Central Pacific islands. The divisions were ordered to detach their infantry group headquarters, one battalion of each infantry regiment (three battalions in total), one artillery battalion, and one engineer company. The 1st EU, which was drawn from the 25th Division and went to Saipan, consisted of four infantry, one mountain-artillery, and one field-artillery battalions plus an engineer company. The 5th EU, sent to garrison Pagan Island in the

A US Marine poses with a captured 7.7mm Type 99 LMG on Saipan, July 13, 1944. Roughly 53,000 Type 99 LMGs were produced, but it never completely supplanted the earlier Type 11 and Type 96 LMGs, both of which fired the less-powerful 6.5×50mm round. (US Marine Corps)

US Coast Guard men examine a knocked-out Type 95 *Ha-Gō* light tank on Peleliu in October 1944 after fighting had moved inland to the Umurbrogol Mountain. Japanese light tanks were considered death traps by Americans who had become accustomed to seeing M4 medium tanks. The small size of the tank is apparent when compared with the men viewing it. (Associated Press/Alamy Stock Photo)

Marianas, was organized from the 71st Division and had two infantry and one mountain-artillery battalions, and one engineer company. The 6th EU, formed from the 1st and 11th divisions and sent to Guam, had six infantry, one field-artillery, and one mountain-artillery battalions, and two engineer companies.

The 31st Army reorganized the three EUs (and other detachments) into IMBs and IMRs in April 1944. The 1st EU on Saipan became the 47th IMB with the 315th, 316th, 317th, and 318th Independent Infantry Battalions (IIBs), an artillery battalion, and an engineer company. On Guam the 6th EU formed the 48th IMB and 10th IMR. The 48th IMB was formed from the 11th Division's units while the 1st Division's detachment formed the 10th IMR. The 48th IMB was composed of the 319th, 320th, 321st, and 322d IIBs along with an artillery unit and an engineer company. The 10th IMR had three infantry battalions, one artillery battalion, and one engineer company. The 5th EU formed the 9th IMR for the defense of Pagan, but its III Battalion was trapped on Saipan and fought there. The 53d IMB was organized in the Palaus out of miscellaneous service and support troops, including unattached sea-transport engineers. The brigade's 346th IIB fought on Peleliu alongside elements of the 14th Division. This IMB included another four IIBs spread throughout the Palaus.

Each IIB in the 31st Army theoretically had three rifle companies, one machine-gun company, and one infantry-gun company with 579 all ranks. Authorized weapons included 318 rifles, 27 grenade launchers, 27 LMGs, 12 HMGs, two 70mm infantry howitzers, and two 37mm antitank guns. On paper an IMB's artillery unit was a battalion of 12 mountain or field guns. The 47th IMB, however, included the uniquely structured 3d Independent Mountain Artillery Regiment (one battalion of 12 75mm mountain guns and crews for 12 150mm howitzers) and the III/10th Field Artillery Regiment (one battery of eight 75mm field guns and two batteries each of seven 105mm howitzers). The 48th IMB had the former III/11th Mountain Artillery Regiment with three batteries of four 75mm mountain guns each. The 53d IMB's artillery unit was formed in the Palaus from miscellaneous personnel with a mix of 75mm mountain and field guns.

DOCTRINE AND TACTICS

US amphibious warfare

US amphibious doctrine during World War II had its origins in the United States' acquisition of the Philippine islands after the Spanish–American War (1898). Growing military forces of the Japanese Empire, combined with their victory in the Russo-Japanese War (1904–05), led US planners to view Japan as the major threat to the Philippines. Following World War I, a League of Nations mandate gave Japan control of Central Pacific islands that had been ruled by Imperial Germany as part of German New Guinea. In a war against the United States, Japan could use these islands to interdict the Central Pacific route that US forces would have to take to reach the Philippines. To counter such developments, the US Navy and US Marine Corps began studying how to seize and defend islands in the Central Pacific. Concepts were developed, beginning with Major Earl H. "Pete" Ellis USMC and his seminal 1921 study titled *Advanced Base Operations in Micronesia.* In this work, Ellis identified possible island and atoll objectives, assessed potential Japanese defenses, and estimated US landing forces needed. Ellis also identified key factors for successful ship-to-shore assaults, including disembarkation of troops from transports into landing boats, organization and control of landing boats as they advanced toward the beach, composition and equipment of combat teams to conduct assaults, and the roles of air and naval-gunfire support, intelligence, and communications. From this beginning, the US Navy and US Marine Corps studied, developed, tested, and refined the art and science of amphibious warfare.

US amphibious-warfare doctrine throughout World War II was based on the 1938 version of Fleet Training Publication 167 (FTP-167), *Landing Operations Doctrine.* Throughout the Pacific War this FTP was continually revised to reflect lessons learned. US amphibious operations in the Solomon Islands and New Guinea during 1942 and 1943 had tested this doctrine during unopposed and lightly resisted landings. Then in late 1943 and early

Troop-carrying LVTs head for a beach in the Marianas. As shown here, additional machine guns were mounted on LVTs. Fully loaded with men and equipment the LVT rode low in the water, requiring that landings be made in low-wave conditions. The number "48" on this LVT indicates the eighth vehicle of the fourth wave. (© CORBIS/ Corbis via Getty Images)

Frontal view of an LVT(A)-4 between actions. The 75mm M2 howitzer provided better firepower to support infantry, especially when attacking fortified positions. These vehicles replaced the earlier 37mm M6 gun-armed LVT(A)-1 by the summer of 1944, before the Marianas and Peleliu invasions. The armor on LVT(A)-4s did not compare to that of the M4A2 medium tanks, however, and M4A2s assumed the infantry-support role ashore as soon as they could be landed. (US Army)

1944 the invasions of the Gilbert and Marshall islands validated the doctrine during opposed amphibious assaults on coral atolls. After each operation, US forces determined lessons learned, identifying what had gone wrong and what needed improvement or changes. From these lessons they developed new equipment, technologies, tactics, techniques, and procedures to remedy the identified shortcomings and to enhance force capabilities.

When Major General Smith commented in his after-action report on the capture of Kwajalein and Eniwetok atolls that "there is still much to be desired to improve planning, improve coordination of efforts and prepare for the attack of more difficult objectives" (quoted in Shaw, Nulty, & Turnbladh 1966: 227), he was looking ahead to invasions of larger volcanic islands such as Saipan, Guam, and Peleliu. On these islands, unlike recently captured atolls, the Japanese would have more space with more rugged terrain in which to deploy and hide. Rather than a few days of fighting, these islands were expected to require weeks to secure.

After Tarawa Atoll, US landing forces used LVTs to carry assault waves across coral reefs instead of small-ramped landing craft. Experience in the Gilberts and Marshalls showed that an assault regiment required the equivalent of a battalion of LVTs. Amtrac battalions, now grouped into a non-divisional asset pool at the corps and force level, were assigned to assault units during the planning phase and execution of invasions. Saipan's D-day, June 15, saw the 2d and 4th Marine divisions each landing two regiments abreast. This assault required eight amtrac battalions (four US Marine Corps and four US Army) with over 700 LVTs. The new LVT-4 was used for the first time. It had a stern-mounted ramp, allowing troops to debark behind the vehicle instead of climbing over the sides while exposed to enemy fire. Additionally, the LVT-4 could carry heavier weapons and jeeps ashore. LVT(A)s made up the first assault wave. Although not tanks, the LVT(A)s could provide ad hoc armor support to infantry until supporting tanks were landed by subsequent waves.

The Tarawa Atoll operation proved that many US Navy officers had overestimated the effectiveness of naval gunfire against land targets. To improve fire support, therefore, the US Navy built replicas of some of

A Stinson OY-1 observation aircraft aboard an escort aircraft carrier. Beginning with the Marianas and Peleliu operations, the Marines assigned an air observation squadron (designated VMO) to each division that flew these lightweight observation and liaison aircraft. They were used for artillery spotting and reconnaissance and sometimes carried ground commanders aloft to view the ground over which their commands would attack. (USN 80-G-378466)

Tarawa Atoll's defensive structures and other defenses on the Kahoolawe range in the Hawaiian Islands. These targets were first used to test the effectiveness of shells and then to train fire-support ships, the performance of which were graded. In order to enhance gunfire effectiveness, US Navy destroyers were stationed as close to the beach as possible. They then tracked the advancing assault waves and only lifted their fire on the beach just as the leading wave reached it. Old battleships were placed within thousands of yards of the beach to deliver pinpoint gunfire on designated targets instead of blindly shelling geographical areas. Landing Craft Infantry (Gun), or LCI(G)s, armed with 40mm and 20mm cannons, .50-caliber HMGs, and 4.5in rockets, approached the reef as close as possible to suppress the enemy as the first wave of landing craft reached the beach. The fleet now risked fire-support ships to support the troops. Before the Marshalls landings, Rear Admiral Richmond K. Turner told his ships' captains: "We expect to lose some ships! If your mission demands it, risk your ship!" (quoted in Shaw, Nulty, & Turnbladh 1966: 124).

Naval-gunfire support was structured around "batteries," defined as two or more guns of the same caliber on the same ship controlled by the same fire-control station. There were four classes of battery. Those tasked with preparation delivered intensive fire on the assault beaches and adjacent positions while the first wave of landing craft approached the beach. Close-support batteries furnished fire in support of units ashore against enemy troops, weapons, or positions which were near the supported troops and posed the most immediate threat to them. Deep-support batteries placed fire on enemy artillery, reserves, or critical points. Batteries tasked with special missions provided deep supporting fire with large-caliber naval guns against targets such as seacoast batteries and heavy permanent fortifications. With their 5in guns and small size, US Navy destroyers were a primary source of close-support batteries. It was common to assign a given destroyer to provide direct support to a particular battalion during an assault, which helped to build teamwork and confidence between ground units and ships.

Underwater Demolition Teams (UDTs) were a wartime innovation. In the Pacific teams were formed after the Tarawa Atoll action, during which

US Marines pose in a front-line position on Saipan, July 1, 1944. The US Marine Corps expected that every Marine was a rifleman before he served in any other capacity. Because all Marines received infantry training, a division was able to use men serving in non-infantry units as replacement riflemen in emergencies and did not have to assign infantry units to protect what other armies considered rear-area units. (USN 80-G-287156)

the presence of the reef forced Marines landing after the first wave to wade ashore from their landing craft. Some tanks were lost when they tried to move from their landing craft to the beach across the reef. Many of the UDT personnel came from the US Navy NCBs and were responsible for initiating the technique of swimming across reefs that became the classic UDT operation. Each UDT consisted of 16 officers and 80 enlisted men. The UDT swimmers performed four principal tasks: pre-assault reconnaissance, sometimes at night, but usually in daylight; pre-assault demolition of underwater obstacles and mines that would otherwise hinder the landings and marking of cleared lanes and channels; guiding LVT waves and landing craft to the beach during the assault; and conducting post-assault blasting of channels across reefs to facilitate the landing of personnel and supplies. Sometimes daylight beach reconnaissance was carried out to deceive the enemy as to the location of the actual assault. Reconnaissance data collected included: reef conditions, including their width, smoothness, and slope at the edges; depths of water over reefs and channels and location of any holes in the reef; surf conditions; tides and currents; the location and nature of obstacles and mines; and the location and description of beach defenses visible from seaward. Daylight UDT missions, frequently carried out in conjunction with pre-invasion minesweeping, were conducted under the cover of dedicated naval gunfire. Detailed fire-support plans were drawn up to support the UDT teams and minesweepers, and large quantities of ammunition were allocated to these fire-support actions. Fires were concentrated on destroying beach defenses and guns.

Unity of command and teamwork were key to the success of an amphibious assault against a defended beach. Doctrine called for a naval attack force under a senior US Navy officer to carry out such an operation. The attack force itself included both the naval forces and a landing force of ground troops. The naval forces included transport, fire-support, escort, and

A US Navy corpsman performs a blood transfusion on a Marine wounded on Saipan. The US Navy provided medical personnel, including corpsmen who served as front-line medics, to US Marine Corps units. Japan's shift to a doctrine of prolonged battles of attrition on Pacific islands resulted in increased US casualties and greater demand for medical support that included corpsmen like this one, doctors, and US Navy hospitals for Marine divisions. (Mondadori via Getty Images)

other ships as well as aircraft. Organized into embarkation groups for loading aboard transports, troops would reorganize once ashore into their normal tactical units for extended land combat. Groups were created around regular tactical organizations such as regiments, battalions, and companies, with attachments and detachments as required. Regimental groups were named Combat Teams (CTs) or Regimental Combat Teams (RCTs), and teams centered on infantry battalions were labeled Battalion Landing Teams (BLTs). Ground commanders were embarked on the flagship with their US Navy counterparts throughout the chain of command to promote teamwork.

Command and communications are complex during a major amphibious operation, but senior naval and ground commanders of the amphibious forces and their staffs no longer used battleships and cruisers as flagships. Instead, they used a special command ship known as an Auxiliary General Command (AGC). The AGCs provided large and reliable communications suites, plenty of staff space, and more accommodation on a ship that was dedicated to command and control independent of other duties. Many US Navy officers had difficulty adjusting to serving on a noncombat auxiliary, but the advantages AGCs offered to command and control, as well as freeing fighting ships to concentrate on providing effective fire support, soon become obvious.

Japanese island defense

In June 1944 Japanese doctrine was characterized by a strong aversion to passive defense. US Intelligence determined that "They apply this concept to defense against amphibious operations ... Their mission is to annihilate the enemy forces before a landing can be effected or as soon after the initial landings as possible" (MID 29 1945). During earlier Central Pacific attacks, US troops faced a substantial, well-prepared defense only at Betio Island within Tarawa Atoll. These defenses were like a hard static shell around Betio, however, which was quickly shattered once pierced. As US forces prepared to invade the Marianas the Japanese planned their defense to "organize the most suitable landing beaches for strong defense, and to cover the intervening coast with mobile and static patrols" (MID 29 1945). The defenders intended to "prevent the landing by superior firepower; but, if the landing actually is made ... defeat it at the water's edge with counterattacks" (MID 29 1945). This approach was articulated on May 10, 1944, in the island-defense plan drawn up by the 1st EU (reorganized as 47th IMB) on Saipan:

> When the enemy elements are attempting to land: The main fire-power will be directed at the enemy landing forces prior to their arrival on the beach. Taking advantage of the confusion, the enemy will be rapidly destroyed by counter attacks, mounted from all sectors wherever the opportunity presents itself.
>
> Should the enemy succeed in gaining a foothold on the beach, intense fire will be concentrated and determined counter-attacks launched with the aid of reserves and tanks. Although the advantages of surprise will be lost, the enemy landing forces can be dealt with by further attacks after night fall. (Quoted in Crowl 1993: 63)

On larger volcanic islands, as opposed to coral atolls, the Japanese were able to deploy artillery in depth. Coastal-defense, antiboat, antitank, and infantry guns were sited to fire on enemy ships and landing craft using direct fire. Mountain and field guns, as well as mortars, were emplaced inland and sited to fire on both the landing beach and the reef in front of it. Frontal and flanking fires were pre-surveyed and markers, including colored flags, placed to cue gunners once enemy landing craft were in range. Fighting positions were to be constructed on high ground immediately behind the beaches in order to dominate the beaches with firepower. If higher ground was not available, fighting positions were placed near the water's edge. The defenders would engage the enemy as he was dealing with beach obstacles and debarking from landing craft before his heavy crew-served weapons became available.

If the US forces established a beachhead, Japanese doctrine called for counterattacking and destroying it. This doctrine included the concept of executing counterlandings, which was one of the motivations for organizing the ocean-type divisions. With two exceptions, these divisions each included an amphibious regiment and an attached shipping engineer regiment. The amphibious regiment was intended to perform the counterlanding role using the self-propelled barges of the shipping engineer regiment.

Japanese forces had executed counterattacks against US beachheads beginning with the Guadalcanal campaign (August 1942–February 1943). Once Marines had captured Guadalcanal's airfield, the Japanese mounted

a series of failed counterattacks; first by one battalion in August, a brigade in September, and a reinforced division in October. Each of these attacks faced a larger and better-equipped US force, however. During 1943 the Japanese launched a failed regimental-size counterattack against a US division attacking Munda on New Georgia Island in the Solomons. In March 1944 the IJA's 17th Army on Bougainville attacked the US lodgment that had been prepared for defense during the preceding four months. Once again the Japanese attackers were outnumbered and outgunned and the attack served only to attrite Japanese strength.

On Saipan and Guam, Japanese troops conducted violent counterattacks after the Marines successfully established beachheads. On both islands these counterattacks allowed the Marines to inflict heavy casualties on the Japanese. The heavy losses among Japan's trained infantry served to help the US forces reduce the garrisons' survivors and capture both islands.

After experiencing repeated failures of beach defenses to stop landings followed by counterattacks that proved unable to destroy US lodgments, the Japanese changed their doctrine of island defense in summer 1944. Repulsing a US assault was no longer the defenders' only objective. Units were ordered to take maximum advantage of natural and manmade fortifications, and to deploy and camouflage weapons, positions, and supplies. Defenses were ordered to be built inland from potential landing beaches to reduce the effects of devastating naval bombardments. Inland defensive positions were to be constructed in depth and sited for mutual protection, thus forcing the US troops to attack under unfavorable conditions. Artillery, mortars, and dual-purpose guns would be hidden and used to harass US forces attempting to use captured portions of an island, such as an airfield. Troops were instructed to avoid exposure to US aerial reconnaissance, bombardment, and naval shelling. While orders still called for defeating the landing at the ocean's shore, garrisons were instructed to preserve their strength and carry out a protracted defense.

Large-scale counterattacks were to be executed only during the first night after a US landing and with the intention of inflicting maximum US casualties. These counterattacks were to be carefully planned, timed, coordinated, and

rehearsed in advance of an invasion. Counterattackers were ordered to take maximum advantage of terrain and obstacles using modern small-unit tactics and infantry skills to reduce Japanese losses. Suicidal *Banzai* charges were not to be executed because it was essential to conserve men and weapons for as long as possible.

Japan's new doctrine essentially conceded that the defenders could not stop US forces from capturing an island from them. In the end, the doctrine actually called for island garrisons to fight to the death while inflicting as many US casualties as possible. On Peleliu, the 1st Marine Division encountered this new doctrine and the battle became a preview of 1945's fights on Iwo Jima and Okinawa.

Entering service in 1932, the 7.7mm Type 92 HMG was a scaled-up version of the 6.5mm Type 3. Strip-fed, it was nicknamed the "Woodpecker" by Allied troops due to its distinctive sound when fired. (INTERFOTO/Alamy Stock Photo)

A 7.7mm Type 92 HMG mounted within a fortified firing position. This machine gun had an effective rate of fire of about 450rd/min, due to its strip-type ammunition feed. The Type 92's effective range on the battlefield was approximately 800yd. Machine guns like these, in well-fortified and camouflaged positions, were important to Japanese island defenses. (Keystone/Getty Images)

Saipan

June 15, 1944

BACKGROUND TO BATTLE

Saipan was defended by IJA and IJN ground troops. The main IJA units were elements of the 43d Division under Lieutenant General Saitō Yoshitsugu (less the I/135th Infantry on Tinian) and 47th IMB (less the 315th IIB on Pagan). The I/18th Infantry (29th Division), rebuilt from survivors of US Navy submarine attacks on transports, the III/9th IMR, and most of the 9th Tank Regiment were also on Saipan. The 43d Division's 118th Infantry Regiment had lost heavily in transit from submarine attacks. Its survivors were merged with other survivors of sunken transports and rebuilt to about 60 percent of authorized manpower, but they were poorly armed. The IJN contributed the 5th Special Base Force (SBF) with the 55th Naval Guard Force (NGF) and 1st Yokosuka SNLF. IJA troops had arrived on Saipan beginning in March 1944. The 43d Division was shipped during late May and early June in two convoys. The first convoy arrived without loss, but five of the seven transports in the second convoy (*Katsukawa Maru*, *Tamahime Maru*, *Takoka Maru*, *Havre Maru*, and *Kashmasan Maru*) were torpedoed and sunk by submarines USS *Shark* (SS-314) and USS *Pintado* (SS-387).

Japanese fortifications were planned to be completed in November 1944, but the US forces advanced faster than anticipated and so these were incomplete when Marines landed on June 15, 1944. The construction of fortifications was hampered by US Navy submarines sinking supply ships carrying much-needed material. A 31st Army report from May 31 stated:

We cannot strengthen the fortifications appreciably now unless we can get materials suitable for permanent construction. Specifically, unless the units are supplied with cement, steel reinforcements for cement, barbed wire, lumber, etc.,

A view of the IJA's 150mm Type 4 howitzer. The Saipan defenders deployed 12 of these howitzers, which fired a 79lb shell; they were centrally located on the island to fire on any of the possible landing beaches. Although Japanese artillery inflicted losses, in the end, it failed to stop the Marines' assault. (US Army)

which cannot be obtained in these islands, no matter how many soldiers there are they can do nothing in regard to fortifications but sit around with their arms folded, and the situation is unbearable. (Quoted in Crowl 1993: 62)

US forces later discovered IJN heavy coastal-defense guns in storage, awaiting the construction of emplacements. Nevertheless, six coastal batteries covered Saipan's western shore, four on the east side, and one on the south side. The Japanese expected a landing on Saipan's west side where Tanapag Harbor and the towns of Tanapag, Garapan, and Charan Kanoa were located, but the defenders still protected the eastern beaches.

Saipan was divided into four sectors: the Northern Sector was held by the 135th Infantry Regiment; the Navy Sector was defended by the 5th SBF and one battalion of the 136th Infantry Regiment; the Central Sector was held by the rest of the 136th Infantry Regiment; and the Southern Sector was defended by the 47th IMB. The 3d Independent Mountain Artillery Regiment and III/10th Field Artillery were deployed in the Southern Sector behind the beaches near Charan Kanoa. This central position allowed the artillery to fire on both east and west coast beaches. The Japanese wanted to stop the landings

Marines inspect an IJN coastal-defense gun after Saipan's capture. Reportedly a 6in piece, this gun was knocked out of action by the US Navy's pre-landing bombardment of Saipan. Old-style open gun emplacements were death traps by 1944. American aerial photography identified any exposed emplacements before the attack began, enabling air bombardment and naval gunfire to destroy or neutralize such positions. (USMC 93094)

Marines bring in two members of the Japanese garrison, Saipan, July 4, 1944. Note the very different shades of uniform worn by the two captives. Both sides found the climatic conditions very challenging. Saipan has a tropical rainforest climate with a year-round average maximum temperature of 84°F, with little seasonal temperature variation. In June the average relative humidity is 79 percent; this results in a heat index (the temperature which the human body experiences) of 94°F. (PhotoQuest/Getty Images)

at the water's edge: "beaches judged best suited for amphibious landings were guarded by powerful forces backed by comparatively feeble local reserves. A short distance inland, the enemy had prepared a second line designed to contain penetrations of the coastal perimeter until a counterattack could be organized" (Shaw, Nalty, & Turnbladh 1966: 260). Battalions defending beaches placed 80 percent of their infantry in shoreline positions, leaving few local reserves. Lieutenant General Saitō's divisional reserve was composed of four rifle companies and the 9th Tank Regiment (less two companies). He also had the survivors of the 118th Infantry Regiment, which had arrived on June 7.

"Softening up" Saipan started on June 11 with an afternoon fighter sweep conducted by TF 58. Over the next three days the carrier-based aircraft of TF 58 flew strikes to destroy or degrade Japanese defenses. On June 13, fast battleships from TF 58 shelled Saipan, but with little result. On June 14 the amphibious forces arrived and their dedicated fire-support ships began a systematic bombardment of Saipan's beaches and installations. This involved: eight old battleships, two with eight 16in guns each and six with 12 14in guns each; six heavy cruisers, each with nine 8in guns; five light cruisers, each with 12 or 15 6in guns; and 26 destroyers armed with 5in guns. This bombardment was significantly more effective than that of the fast battleships. According to Marine Corps artillery expert Major Robert D. Heinl: "The reason for this was no mystery; these ships had devoted considerable time to shore bombardment, both in training and battle experience. During the rehearsals at Kahoolawe, a month prior to the operation, the old battleships had received valuable experience. They knew the necessity of slow, painstaking adjustment" (quoted in Hoffman 1950: 40).

On June 15, the 2d and 4th Marine divisions assaulted Saipan on a two-division front. Each division landed two regiments side by side. To the north, the 2d Marine Division landed in the Central Sector with (north to south) 6th and 8th Marines and 2d Marines in reserve. To the south of the 2d Marine Division the 4th Marine Division landed the 23d and 25th Marines (north to south) in the Southern Sector. Each regiment landed two battalions abreast, each battalion deploying two companies up front and one behind. The divisions' zones were separated by an 800yd gap.

The 23d Marines, commanded by Colonel Louis R. Jones, was reinforced by: two companies of US Army 75mm M2 howitzer-armed LVT(A)-4s (34 vehicles); Cos. B and C with 29 M4A2s and Co. D (less one platoon) with 12 M3A1 flamethrower tanks and four M5A1 light tanks of the 4th Marine Tank Battalion; combat engineers of Co. C, 20th Marines; and support units. This force, designated RCT23, landed BLT 3 (3/23d Marines) on Beach Blue 1 and BLT 2 (2/23d Marines) on Beach Blue 2. BLT 1 (1/23d Marines) was the regimental reserve. The regiment was lifted in 125 LVT-2s, 21 LVT-4s, 58 Landing Craft, Vehicle, Personnel (LCVPs), and 34 Landing Craft Mechanized (LCMs). Medium-tank companies, flamethrower tanks, and the regimental 75mm SPMs were carried in LCMs. The assault battalions were organized in seven waves: the first wave used 17 LVT(A)-4s, the second through fifth waves had 12 LVT-2s or LVT-4s, and the sixth and seventh waves used LCVPs.

The landing was planned as "a blitz amphibious assault, continuous from the shipboard to the first high ground more than a mile inland from the beach (O-1 line)" (RCT23 SAR 1944). Plans called for waves 1, 2, and 3 to advance inland to the O-1 line and then unload their troops and establish the beachhead perimeter. LVT(A)-4s would deploy along the O-1 line and provide fire support for the Marines. The troop-carrying LVTs of waves 2 and 3 were to return to the water, take on troops and equipment from the LCVP waves then land these on the beach. While this was in progress, the LVTs of waves 4 and 5 would stop on the beach and discharge their men. These troops would mop up bypassed resistance.

This aerial photograph of Saipan's invasion beaches was taken during the US naval bombardment before the landing. Saipan, the largest of the Northern Mariana Islands, is about 12 miles wide at its longest north–south axis and has a maximum east–west axis of 5.6 miles. The island has a land area of 44.55 square miles. In this image, smoke rises from targets that have been shelled. The white areas in the ocean to the right are the offshore reefs. To the left are the rising hills that were the Marines' first-day objectives. (USN 80-G-238385)

1 *c.*0815hrs: Four minutes after leaving the line of departure, 3,000yd offshore, RCT23's first assault waves come under heavy fire from Japanese 75mm, 105mm, and 150mm artillery of the 3d Independent Mountain Artillery Regiment and III/10th Field Artillery, firing from their positions east of Mount Fina Susu. US intelligence subsequently determines that 30 75mm field pieces, 16 105mm howitzers, and eight 150mm howitzers shelled the 2d and 4th Marine divisions' beaches on D-day.

2 0840hrs: Wave 1 (LVT(A)-4s) reaches the shoreline.

3 0845–0907hrs: Waves 2, 3, 4, and 5 reach the beach at six- and eight-minute intervals under intense Japanese artillery and mortar fire. Japanese infantry offer little resistance on and immediately behind the beaches.

4 *c.*0910hrs: Eight troop-carrying LVTs and three LVT(A)-4s with boat teams from the 3/23d Marines move inland as planned toward the O-1 line. The swampy terrain channelizes US movement to a road in single file.

5 *c.*0915hrs: A detachment of five LVT(A)-4s and three LVTs with troops of the 2/23d Marines move forward toward the O-1 line. Terrain restricts these vehicles to the Aslito Road.

6 0930hrs: Most of the 2/23d and 3/23d Marines are scattered and disorganized on the beach because of intense Japanese artillery and mortar fire. The shelling and adverse inland terrain prevent the planned US blitz to the O-1 line.

7 1000hrs: Elements of the 2/23d and 3/23d Marines reach the O-1 line. The 3/23d Marines' detachment secure Mount Fina Susu. Both detachments lack flank support.

8 1055hrs: The 1/23d Marines lands on Beach Blue 1.

9 1135hrs: Elements of the 3/23d Marines on Mount Fina Susu are pinned down by heavy Japanese artillery fire.

10 *c.*1200hrs: Small groups of Japanese infantry attempt to surround Marines on Mount Fina Susu. Fighting continues on and off through the afternoon.

11 1300–1700hrs: The 2/23d Marines detachment skirmishes with elements of the 47th IMB on the O-1 line.

12 1745hrs: Marine detachments on the O-1 line are ordered to withdraw to their battalion lines before dark.

13 1900hrs: RCT23 prepares to hold a beachhead 300–500yd inland of Beaches Blue 1 and 2 during the night.

Battlefield environment

Compared to coral atolls Saipan is a larger land area, with multiple types of topography and vegetation. Troops had to fight through mangrove swamps, sugarcane fields, sizable towns that required house-to-house fighting, up and down volcanic ridges, and had to secure mountain caves. About 70 percent of Saipan was cultivated as sugarcane fields. These fields impeded foot movement, limited fields of fire, and provided excellent concealment.

None of the beaches on Saipan was ideal for an amphibious landing. The Americans selected the western side of the island because it had sufficient beaches to allow two divisions to land side by side, and the terrain here slopes up gently from sandy beaches. The beaches are, however, behind barrier reefs that cover the west side of the island, with only a small gap in the reef in front of the town of Charan Kanoa, which was just inland of the 3/23d Marines' landing beach. Just inland of the assault beaches was a large area of swamp centered on the fresh waters of Lake Susupe, which channelized movement to roads and tracks. About 1.1 miles inland of the landing beaches was a ridgeline averaging about 140ft in height. The ridgeline was the planned objective line for D-day. Along it ridge and east of Charan Kanoa was Mount Fina Susu with a height just under 200ft.

One of Saipan's beaches on D+1. Three stalled or damaged LVT(A)-4s are visible on the left. The beach is littered with boxes and cases for supplies that were quickly dropped on the beach during D-day for the assault troops to make use of their contents. Most of these supplies were ammunition and water that were required as soon as possible. Once the shore party was ashore, supply dumps and a regular distribution system were quickly established. (USMC 88365)

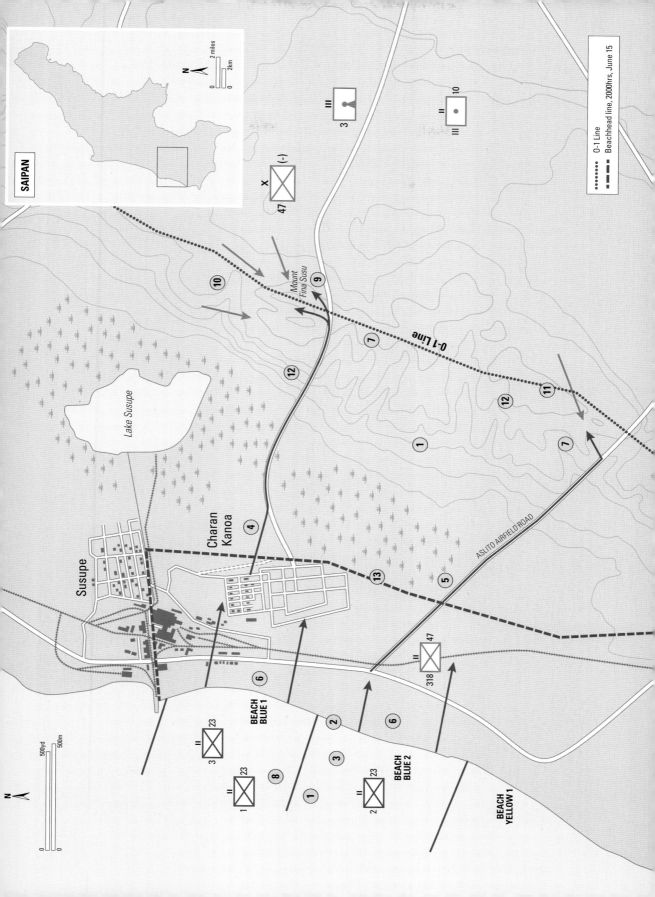

SAIPAN

N

0   2 miles

0   2km

III

3

II

III

10

X

47 (-)

10

Mount
Fina Susu

9

7

0-1 Line

12

12

11

1

7

Lake Susupe

Susupe

Charan
Kanoa

4

13

5

ASLITO AIRFIELD ROAD

Susupe

6

II 47

318

6

2

II 23

3

BEACH
BLUE 1

II 23

1

8

3

1

II 23

2

BEACH
BLUE 2

BEACH
YELLOW 1

N

500yd

500m

0-1 Line

Beachhead line, 2000hrs, June 15

INTO COMBAT

At 0811hrs, RCT23's first assault waves were dispatched from the line of departure, 3,000yd offshore. Between the line of departure and the reef, battleships USS *Tennessee* (BB-43) and USS *California* (BB-44), heavy cruiser USS *Indianapolis* (CA-35), light cruiser USS *Birmingham* (CL-62), and destroyers USS *Bailey* (DD-492), USS *Robinson* (DD-562), USS *Coghlan* (DD-606), USS *Albert W. Grant* (DD-649), USS *Halsey Powell* (DD-696), USS *Norman Scott* (DD-690), and USS *Monssen* (DD-798), were stopped or anchored off the landing beaches. According to Admiral Turner, writing in a letter of January 4, 1950, "this was the first time the Close Support firing vessels had been anchored, or stopped, very close to the beaches, to shore ward of the Line of Departure ... whose average distance from the beach was 2,500 yards" (quoted in Hoffman 1950: 47). These ships bombarded the beaches, enfilading flanks, and enemy positions inland. Off RCT23's Blue beaches were *Birmingham*, *Indianapolis*, and *Norman Scott*. A total of 24 LCI(G)s, three for each landing beach, were assigned to bombard each beach just before the first assault waves landed. As these LCI(G)s moved into their firing positions and the US Navy ships shifted their fire from the landing beaches to the O-1 line, Japanese artillery and mortars opened fire on the reef with shells bursting around the armored and troop-carrying LVTs of the leading waves. Marines reported colored flags on the reef that appeared to be registration points for the enemy's guns.

In addition to guns near the beach, heavy artillery fire came from 75mm, 105mm, and 150mm howitzers of the 3d Independent Mountain Artillery Regiment and III/10th Field Artillery firing from positions on high ground east of Charan Kanoa. When the LVTs approached closer to the beaches, Japanese automatic cannons, antitank guns, infantry guns, and machine guns joined the firing. Wave 1's LVT(A)-4s slowed down and some stopped on the reef while under Japanese fire. As Wave 2's LVT-2s caught up with the LVT(A)-4s, the armored amphibians resumed their advance through the fire to crawl onto the beach at 0840hrs. Many LVT(A)-4s stopped on the beach having moved only 25yd from the water, and started to engage any Japanese positions they could see. Wave 2's LVTs hit the beach at 0845hrs, followed by Wave 3 at 0851hrs, Wave 4 at 0859hrs, and Wave 5 at 0907hrs. Despite the shelling, only a few LVTs were hit while traveling toward the beach. The congregation of LVT(A)-4s on the beach engaging the Japanese defenders caused delays among the US forces as troop-carrying LVTs had to maneuver around them to find suitable debarkation positions. Both BLTs became scattered and disorganized because of intense artillery and mortar fire on the approaches and the beach itself. This heavy shelling combined with terrain inland of the Blue beaches prevented the planned speedy US advance to the O-1 line.

In Lieutenant Colonel John J. Cosgrove's 3/23d Marines' zone, eight troop-carrying LVTs and three LVT(A)-4s moved inland as planned toward the O-1 line. The vehicles found swampy terrain channelized movement to a road in single file. These Marines reached the O-1 line at Mount Fina Susu after overcoming minor opposition from a few Japanese riflemen on their way. Once on Mount Fina Susu the Americans came under heavy fire from artillery, firing at ranges between 500yd and 700yd, along with heavy mortar and machine-gun fire. Small groups of Japanese infantry were seen trying to surround the Marines. Without friendly units on either flank, Marines on Mount Fina Susu were ordered to withdraw to the battalion lines before dark. The rest of Cosgrove's battalion debarked on the beach under heavy artillery fire. Some Marines cleared out defenders from trenches and fighting posts on and near the beach. Others started to clear the town of Charan Kanoa.

Beach congestion on Saipan, June 15, 1944. The planned blitz toward the O-1 line, to be conducted by LVT(A)-4s and troop-carrying LVTs, failed largely due to the unexpected terrain encountered on and behind the beach. With most of the LVTs forced to stop on the beach, their troops debarked and unloaded the vehicles. Congestion became a problem on the beaches and Japanese mortar and artillery fire caused casualties. Behind the Marines, LVTs are stopped on the beach and out to sea some of the small support vessels – what appears to be a patrol craft, likely one of the control vessels for the landing, and an LCI(G) gunboat – are visible. (USMC 81840)

Marine riflemen pictured on Saipan. This photograph was probably posed following the capture of a Japanese position in the hills. The enemy bodies in the foreground and the Marine in the background looking through binoculars suggest the Japanese were not returning fire at the time. (Keystone/Getty Images)

Meanwhile, the 2/23d Marines under Lieutenant Colonel Edward J. Dillon landed on Beach Blue 2. LVTs landing in the center of the beach encountered a 4–5ft embankment rising nearly vertically; an obstacle that stopped the LVTs in their tracks. Inland to the southeast of Charan Kanoa was more swampy ground, which restricted vehicles to the Aslito Road. Five LVT(A)-4s and three troop-carrying LVTs with troops of the 2/23d Marines used this road to reach the O-1 line. No more troops of the 2/23d Marines reached the O-1 line on D-day, however. Most of the 2/23d Marines' LVTs stopped 100–200yd inland and debarked their troops. Japanese artillery and mortars were shelling the beach, frequently targeting LVTs. Fighting was conducted by the debarked LVT boat teams without pausing to reorganize into their parent formations. Once again, US Marine Corps training shone as "leaders organized whatever men were nearby, regardless of unit affiliation, and pressed the attack" (Hoffman 1950: 59).

Both Blue beaches were under heavy shelling that inevitably caused losses. Japanese gunners were doing their utmost to defeat the Marines. As they crossed the reef and approached the shore, LVTs were targeted, then once on the beach both LVTs and debarked troops were engaged. Marines later determined that 30 75mm field pieces, 16 105mm howitzers, and eight 150mm howitzers shelled both divisions' beaches on D-day. Many of the 4th Marine Division's casualties suffered on D-Day and D+1 were caused by Japanese artillery. The 4th Marine Division's intelligence officer, Lieutenant Colonel Gooderham L. McCormick, described these afterward:

They were all well placed, with excellent fields of fire and artful concealment. Crew's quarters and ammunition were all below ground ... Entrances were

invariably well back on the reverse slope. Wall diagrams in observation posts marked registration points on the reefs, the channels, the beach lines, roads and intersections adjacent to the beach. These points [the targeted points] were interdicted long after the O.P.'s [observation posts] had been rendered inoperative. (Quoted in Hoffman 1950: 60)

Saipan was proving a tougher fight than that on Roi Island within Kwajalein Atoll in the Marshalls in early February 1944.

The Japanese infantry on the Blue beaches were from the 318th IIB of the 47th IMB. The 318th IIB was formed on Saipan from the III/40th Infantry when the 1st EU reorganized into the 47th IMB. The defenders were first identified by the US forces as the III/40th Infantry from bodies, uniforms, and documents found on the beaches. Throughout the battle, intelligence officers frequently identified original units of the 1st EU as being present. This situation was aggravated when interrogated prisoners, frequently unaware of the reorganizations, identified themselves as belonging to their original unit.

By 0930hrs, RCT23 recorded that its position ashore was "none too favorable; both assault BLTs reported receiving heavy artillery and mortar fire, BLT 2 units on the right had advanced about 150 yards inland, while BLT 3 on the left about 300 yards. At 0932, the reserve BLT was alerted to land on signal and assist the advance of BLT 3" (RCT23 SAR 1944: 32). About this same time, Colonel Jones was asked by the 4th Marine Division if it was feasible to start landing the divisional artillery on the Blue beaches. He informed the division that his RCT had not gained sufficient distance inland to permit the artillery to land and deploy, and recommended delaying the

US Marines take shelter behind an M4A2 medium tank on Saipan. Note the use of a camouflage jacket by the radio operator. Close cooperation between infantry and tanks was critical in combat. Marine divisions each had their own tank battalion that trained with the division's infantry. This fostered teamwork and mutual trust between infantry and tankers. In contrast, the US Army infantry divisions had to rely on attached tank battalions that could be transferred away from the division by higher headquarters. (Corporal Angus Robertson/US Marine Corps/FPG/Hulton Archive/Getty Images)

Securing the beachhead

On D day, June 15, 1944, the Marines planned to secure a beachhead on Saipan based on a ridge line about 1.1 miles inland of the landing beaches. Only a few small detachments were able to reach this line, however, one of which, consisting of eight troop-carrying LVTs and three LVT(A)-4s carrying boat teams of the 3/23d Marines, reached Mount Fina Susu, overlooking the landing beaches. By 1500hrs it was clear that this small force was unsupported on either flank and Japanese troops from the 47th IMB were beginning to outflank them. On the right, an M1919A4 light-machine-gun team fires upon two advancing Japanese squads seeking to outflank the Marines on the ridge line; several Marines carry ammunition cases toward the LMG. The flexibility of the US Marine Corps' 13-man rifle squad organized into three four-man fire-teams is displayed: two fire-teams have taken prone firing positions around their M1918A2 BAR while the third is moving under their squad leader's direction to extend the line to the left. The .50-caliber Browning M2 HMG on the LVT in the foreground is manned by a member of the boat team assigned to the vehicle, as three more boat-team members unload ammunition. Supporting these Marines is a 75mm M2 howitzer-armed LVT(A)-4, which is also firing its top-mounted M2 HMG. Before nightfall, the Marines on Mount Fina Susu and other small detachments will be recalled and ordered to rejoin their parent units nearer the beaches.

artillery until his tanks had been landed and his regiment secured a deeper beachhead. By 1000hrs, RCT23 learned that two small groups of LVT(A)-4s and troop-carrying LVTs of BLTs 2 and 3 had reached positions at the O-1 line, but were stopped and lacked flanking supports.

By 1040hrs, RCT23's situation appeared a little better. Two small detachments had reached the O-1 line, one company of the 3/23d Marines was 300yd inland, and one company was mopping up Charan Kanoa and the immediate beach. The 2/23d Marines had pushed 500yd inland but were now stopped by mortar and machine-gun fire from high ground in front of it. At 1055hrs the reserve BLT, 1/23d Marines under Lieutenant Colonel Ralph Haas, started landing on Beach Blue 1 and was completely ashore by 1135hrs. Because BLTs 2 and 3 could not reach the O-1 line in force, the regiment ordered BLT 1 to disembark on the beach and advance inland on foot. Only its LVTs carrying 81mm mortars and ammunition would remain ashore with the troops; the rest would return to the amphibious force to bring ashore more troops and supplies. BLT 1 cleared any enemy stragglers and assembled 300yd inland to await instructions. This battalion reported receiving mortar and artillery fire. So far, RCT23 had encountered few Japanese infantry; instead, it was facing intense heavy weapons' fire, much of it from well-concealed positions inland.

The need to get tanks ashore to support the riflemen was clear to the US planners. Therefore, tanks were to land on D-day when ordered to do so by commanders of infantry regiments and battalions. On D-day, each 23d Marines assault BLT had a medium-tank company attached: Co. B, 4th Tank Battalion, was assigned to BLT 3 and Co. C, 4th Tank Battalion, to BLT 2. Co. A, 4th Tank Battalion, was assigned to RCT25, landing on the Yellow beaches south of RCT23. Two options were selected for landing tanks based on UDT divers' reports. The first was to send the tank-carrying LCMs through the channel in the reef off Beach Blue 1 and debark the tanks on the beach. The second was to beach the LCMs on the reef and have the tanks move ashore by crossing the reef under their own power. Unfortunately, problems were encountered with both options: "First, the channel was intermittently interdicted by heavy mortar and artillery fire, making movement through it hazardous. And second, in regard to the reef landings, heavy swells had built up by early afternoon, making it difficult to beach LCM's ... Difficulties notwithstanding, the 4th Tank Battalion endeavored to land throughout the afternoon. It was a costly operation" (Hoffman 1950: 60).

Co. B's losses began as its LCMs left the Landing Ship Dock (LSD) transporting the company. One tank was lost when its LCM immediately sank due to a hole in the hull that was inflicted during the disembarkation. An LCM carrying a tank loaded from a cargo ship by crane ended up listing. At 1110hrs Co. B was ordered to land its remaining 13 tanks on Beach Blue 1 in waves of three; the first tanks landed at 1153hrs. The company's report describes its landing:

> The third platoon leader with two more of his tanks proceeded through the Charan-Kanoa channel under heavy enemy artillery fire and landed 20 yards south of the Charan-Kanoa pier, fording about 2 and 1/2 ft of water for a distance of 30 yards, Navy control, mindful of the artillery fire received by the first wave, ordered the next wave to land on the barrier reef south of the channel. The second wave, the remaining 3rd platoon tank and the two Headquarters tanks including the company commander, landed on the reef and proceeded through the lagoon in column fording from 4 to 8 feet of water for 700 yards. The lead tank fell into a "pot-hole" 10 yards from the beach and drowned out. All attempts to tow this tank on to the beach failed and it was abandoned by the crew. This wave received artillery fire also, but not as intense as the first wave had received.
>
> At the time the 2nd wave of tanks landed on the reef, the LCM loaded, with a dangerous list received a direct hit from enemy artillery fire, setting it on fire ... Navy control then sent the next six tanks to 2nd Division's Green Beach. The tanks were landed on the reef and proceeded towards Green Beach Two, some 1100 yards away. There were two columns, each led by a man. In about the center of the lagoon they encountered very deep water. A few tanks were completely submerged and all but one had to be abandoned. One man was killed leading the tanks ashore. The crews of the abandoned tanks joined the 2nd Division as infantry on the beach. The one tank that reached the beach was held by the 2nd Tank Battalion and not allowed to proceed South to join this Company.
>
> ... Navy control was responsible for the loss of five tanks during the landing.
> (Co. B 4th Tank Battalion, *Combat Report*, August 25, 1944: 2)

Instead of 14 M4A2s in support on D-day, BLT 3 found itself with just six, one of which was soon out of action due to saltwater shorting the electrical system.

Co. C's landing was less eventful. At about 0900hrs its commander, Captain Robert C. Neiman, received orders from BLT 2 to land on Beach Blue 2, but it took him nearly two hours to get permission from the US Navy control officer to land. While delayed, Co. C learned from UDT divers that the coral reef of adjacent Beach Yellow 2 offered the tanks a better path to the beach. Just before noon, the LCMs carrying the tanks reached the reef where Co. C debarked its 14 M4A2s in 5½ft of water and drove across 800yd of coral to the beach. The M4A2s drove to an assembly area just inland of Beach Blue 2 where they received orders to advance to the O-1 line

> with their right flank on the road running from Beach Blue 1 to Aslito Airfield. The tanks proceeded to do this, but those tanks not actually on the road began to bog down completely and had to be abandoned under fire. After this the tanks pushed to the O-1 in a column along the road. However, when it was apparent that no infantry was supporting the tanks, they returned to our lines after briefly shelling the O-1 ridge line. (Co. C 4th Tank Battalion, *Combat Report*, August 20, 1944: 1)

With tanks and BLT 1 ashore, RCT23's advanced command post was established ashore 200yd inland of Beach Blue 2 at 1305hrs. Heavy Japanese artillery and mortar fire continued, and caused most casualties. Colonel Jones came ashore around 1500hrs. Most of RCT23 was ashore; artillery was landing and deploying to fire. BLT 1 was on the left protecting the open flank between the 2d and 4th Marine divisions; BLT 2 was 500yd inland and stopped by heavy machine-gun and mortar fire; BLT 3 had a weak hold on part of the O-1 line and was holding the left of the beachhead. Casualties were 16 officers and 904 enlisted.

Troops on the O-1 line were recalled at 1745hrs and RCT23 went on the defense for the night. The 23d Marines had seized a beachhead short of the O-1 line with a depth of 300–500yd. During the night Japanese artillery continued to shell the beaches heavily. No organized counterattack was made against the 4th Marine Division; instead, small parties tried to infiltrate positions, but were either stopped by the front line or mopped up by troops in the rear. VAC was ashore and in force on Saipan by nightfall on June 15. This Japanese effort to stop a US amphibious assault at the water's edge had failed, but the bloody fighting continued until Saipan was declared secure on July 9, 1944.

A Marine M3A1 "Satan" flamethrower light tank in action on Saipan. The flamethrower-equipped tank became increasingly valuable as US troops confronted well-fortified Japanese positions, including those built in caves. Unlike the coral atolls of the Gilberts and Marshalls, the volcanic islands of the Marianas and the uplifted coral mass of Peleliu contained many caves. Capturing these positions could result in heavy casualties for the attackers. (USMC 7160583407)

Guam

July 26, 1944

BACKGROUND TO BATTLE

Directing Guam's ground defense was Lieutenant General Takashina Takeshi, commanding the 29th Division. From his division he had five infantry battalions, although two were under strength, and one 75mm mountain-artillery battalion. Also under his command were the 48th IMB (commanded by Major General Shigematsu Toyashi with four IIBs and one artillery battalion) and the 10th IMR (less one infantry battalion and one artillery battery). Also present was the IJN's 54th NGF. The best estimate of Japanese field and mountain artillery was provided by IIIAC Intelligence based on an August 10 count of captured and destroyed weapons that totaled six 105mm howitzers and 38 75mm mountain and field guns. Not included in this count were 70mm infantry howitzers, antitank guns, and antiaircraft pieces. Takashina had 11 infantry and three artillery battalions to pit against IIIAC's 24 infantry and 13 artillery battalions (48 75mm pack howitzers, 60 105mm howitzers, 36 155mm howitzers, and 12 155mm guns).

On W-day, July 21, IIIAC attacked Guam. The 3d Marine Division landed on beaches between Adelup Point and Asan Point. The 3d Marines landed with two battalions abreast and one in reserve. In the center the 21st Marines landed in a column of battalions, as did the 9th Marines on the left. Asan town was immediately behind the 21st Marines' beach. Opposing the 3d Marine Division were the 320th IIB with other detachments. To the south, the 1st Provisional Marine Brigade landed more than 6nmi south in Agat Bay. Both landings were on the west coast of Guam. IIIAC described W-day as: "Landings successful on all beaches. ... Troops landed against light opposition. Initial opposition consisted mainly of mortar fire directed at boats and landing beaches. Enemy withdrew after brief resistance. No large enemy

A UDT's explosive charge blows up an underwater obstacle off Agat Beach, Guam, before the US invasion of that island, July 1944. Clearing obstacles was dangerous but necessary so LVTs and landing craft could reach the beach. (USN 80-G-700639)

force encountered. Scattered rifle and machine gun fire plus mortar fire received by advancing units. Troops, tanks, and artillery landed approximately as scheduled" (III Amphibious Corps, September 3, 1944: 427).

During the next four days the 3d Marine Division expanded the Asan beachhead. Heavy fighting occurred on the division's east flank where the 3d Marines battled strong opposition between the coast at Adelup Point and the Fonte Plateau. The other two regiments met lighter resistance. During July 22–24, the 3d Marines suffered heavily, especially the 1/3d Marines. This battalion was placed in divisional reserve and relieved by the 2/9th Marines early on July 25.

Later on July 25, the 3d Marine Division renewed its attack. The 3/3d and 2/3d Marines gained 100–300yd of ground toward Agana. Against heavy resistance, the 2/9th Marines (under command of the 3d Marines) advanced nearly 500yd toward the top of the Fonte Plateau. The 2/21st Marines advanced its left flank, in contact with the 2/9th Marines, while its center and right flank advanced just short of the Mount Tenjo Road west of the Fonte Plateau. The 1/21st Marines, in the 21st Marines' center, reached the Mount Tenjo Road after heavy fighting but was driven back across the road by artillery fire from hidden Japanese guns. The 1/21st Marines, with supporting M4A2 medium tanks, inflicted heavy casualties on the opposing infantry. On the 21st Marines' right, the 3/21st Marines succeeded in advancing about 800yd against light resistance, which resulted in an interval opening between the battalion and the 1/21st Marines on its left. On the 3d Marine Division's right flank, the 9th Marines (less the 2/9th Marines) advanced more than 1 mile against light opposition. During this day's fighting, the Japanese facing the 3d and 21st Marines launched numerous local counterattacks to try to restore their positions and hold key terrain. The 3d Marine Division's July 25 evening report to IIIAC listed its casualties since July 20 as 315 dead, 1,760 wounded, and 132 missing. Most of these were from its three infantry regiments.

The inability of Japanese beach defenses and his local counterattacks to stop the Marines caused Lieutenant General Takashina on July 23 to order a coordinated all-out counterattack to drive the Marines back into the ocean. Two days were required to prepare the counterattack, which was scheduled to take place during the night of July 25/26. Takashina planned to use as many troops and as much artillery as possible. To replace combat losses, service and support troops, as well as walking wounded, were incorporated into infantry units to bolster their numbers. The Japanese concentrated from the coast near Adelup Point, through the Fonte Plateau to "Mount Mangan," the name the Japanese

Marines scramble over the sides of an LVT-2 on one of Guam's invasion beaches on July 21, 1944. This technique for debarking from an LVT increased the troops' vulnerability to enemy small-arms and machine-gun fire. To reduce this risk, the newer LVT-4 was equipped with a ramp in its rear that allowed the Marines to debark and shelter behind the vehicle. (USN 80-G-238988)

An LVT-2 can be seen on the beach as Marines take cover on an invasion beach during initial landings on Guam on July 21, 1944. Marines are reorganizing after landing before moving inland and attacking Japanese defenders in the immediate vicinity. This was the most vulnerable time in an amphibious assault. Notice the damaged trees and shredded vegetation caused by the pre-landing naval gunfire. (USN 80-G-239023)

gave the 100ft hill about 1,500yd southwest of the Fonte Plateau. Takashina set up his command post in a cave about 325yd west of Fonte village, while Major General Shigematsu placed his 48th IMB headquarters at Mangan Quarry about 540yd west of Fonte.

On the Japanese west flank, from the coast inland for about 1,000yd, the 54th NGF, reinforced by two IJA tank companies (2d Company, 9th Tank Regiment, and the 29th Division Tank Company), was to attack toward Asan. Assembled in front of the Fonte Plateau was the 10th IMR (less one battalion), which served as the main effort for the 48th IMB. Elements of the brigade's 319th IIB and remnants of the 320th and 321st IIBs attacked along with the attached 10th IMR. The brigade's objective was the high ground near Adelup Point. Colonel Ohashi Hikoshiro assembled his 18th Infantry Regiment (less I Battalion) in the hills south of Afana. Ohashi's regiment was Takashina's main attack force. It was to attack down the hills toward Asan Point and capture the high ground overlooking the beaches. On the 18th Infantry Regiment's left, one company from the 10th IMR was to attack along the Tatqua River and guard the western flank of the 18th Infantry Regiment. Among the attackers were small special detachments armed with demolition charges; these detachments were ordered to bypass infantry defenses and instead try to blow up artillery pieces, supply dumps, and vehicles. A US Marine Corps study later concluded, "In contrast to the disjointed, unorganized, banzai charges that Marines had encountered throughout the Pacific fighting, Takashina had planned a coordinated counterattack by the defenders" (Lodge 1954: 79). Unfortunately for the Japanese, many of their veteran infantrymen, soldiers who had come to Guam from the IJA's 1st and 11th Infantry divisions, were killed or wounded before the counterattack started.

1 *c.***0000hrs:** The 10th IMR (less one battalion) and elements of the 48th IMB (parts of the 319th and 320th IIBs) launch the first of seven major counterattacks against the 2/9th Marines.

2 **0030hrs:** Japanese infantry – an unidentified company of the 10th IMR – force a detachment of the 3d Marine Division's reconnaissance company out of the gap between the 21st and 9th Marines.

3 *c.***0030hrs:** The III/18th Infantry launches probing counterattacks along the 3/21st Marines' front.

4 **0100hrs:** Using the 217th and 218th Construction battalions as improvised infantry, the 54th NGF assaults the 2/3d and 3/3d Marines. Repeated assaults occur before dawn and are all repulsed.

5 **0100hrs:** Elements of the 48th IMB (the 321st IIB plus other detachments) assault the 2/21st Marines. These counterattacks continue during the night until dawn.

6 **0400hrs:** The II/18th Infantry counterattacks the 1/21st Marines' positions.

7 **0400hrs:** The III/18th Infantry assaults the 3/21st Marines' lines.

8 **0500hrs:** Repulsed, the III/18th Infantry then moves along the 3/21st Marines' front line and find and attack through the gap between the 3/21st Marines and the 9th Marines on its right.

9 **0530hrs:** Headquarters 3/21st Marines comes under heavy attack. US headquarters personnel form a defensive perimeter and cipher equipment is buried.

10 *c.***0600hrs:** Around dawn, the Japanese launch a seventh and last attack on the 2/9th Marines, which is nearly out of ammunition, just as a platoon of M4A2 tanks arrives and engages the Japanese. In minutes, a second tank platoon arrives, escorting trucks carrying ammunition.

11 **0615hrs:** Co. L, 9th Marines attacks Japanese troops in the gap and restores contact with the 3/21st Marines.

12 **0630hrs:** The 1/21st Marines begins a counterattack with tank support.

13 **0630hrs:** Japanese infiltrators assault the 3d Marine Division's hospital, which is defended by wounded Marines and medical personnel.

14 **0900hrs:** Fighting ends in the 2/9th Marines' sector and the bodies of 950 Japanese are found. US intelligence subsequently reports that the 10th IMR has been reduced to about 100 effectives.

15 **1200hrs:** The 3d Marine Division's lines are restored; the Japanese counterattacks are over.

Battlefield environment

Located about 100nmi south of Saipan, Guam is the southernmost and largest of the Marianas. The island has an area of 212 square miles. It is about 30 miles in length with a width of 8½ miles at the northern tip and a maximum width in the south of 11½ miles. The island is fringed by coral reefs that vary between 25yd and 700yd wide. The deepest reefs are covered by about 2ft of water at high tide and required the use of amphibious tractors for an amphibious assault.

Guam is of volcanic origin and is divided into a northern limestone plateau, a center of low hills, and a southern area of volcanic hills. In July 1944 the northern part of Guam was heavily covered with tropical forests, weeds, trailing vines, lianas, and underbrush. The mountaintops were mainly barren volcanic rock featuring only sparse growths of scrub. The southern part of the island was mostly covered with sword, cogon, and bunch grass plus scrub forest. Between Mount Alifan and Mount Lamlam there were stands of timber, however.

The northern part of Guam's coast has steep cliffs that rise as much as 600ft above sea level and is the source of most of the island's freshwater. In the southern part of the island part of the coast also has shoreline cliffs that are lower but still prevented an amphibious assault. The southern and southeast coasts have heavy surf conditions that ruled them out of use for a landing. On Guam's western side, however, there were about 15 miles of coastline suitable for an amphibious assault. These beaches were located north and south of the Orote Peninsula and were less than 3,000ft from either cliffs or hills. The beaches used by the 3d Marine Division on D-day were generally within 1,000yd or less of the 200ft elevation contour line. Along these beaches the fringing reefs could easily be crossed by LVTs. Once ashore, the beaches were wide enough and deep enough to permit assault waves to land, reorganize, and establish a beachhead before moving forward to tackle the hilly and mountainous terrain inland.

As with most tropical islands in the Western Pacific, the weather on Guam is warm throughout the year with less humidity from November through March. July's mean monthly temperature near sea level is 83.3°F with a mean relative humidity of 87 percent, which results in a heat index of 95°F. Large supplies of drinking water are required for humans working, or fighting, in this level of heat. July through December is Guam's wet season during which it rains almost every day.

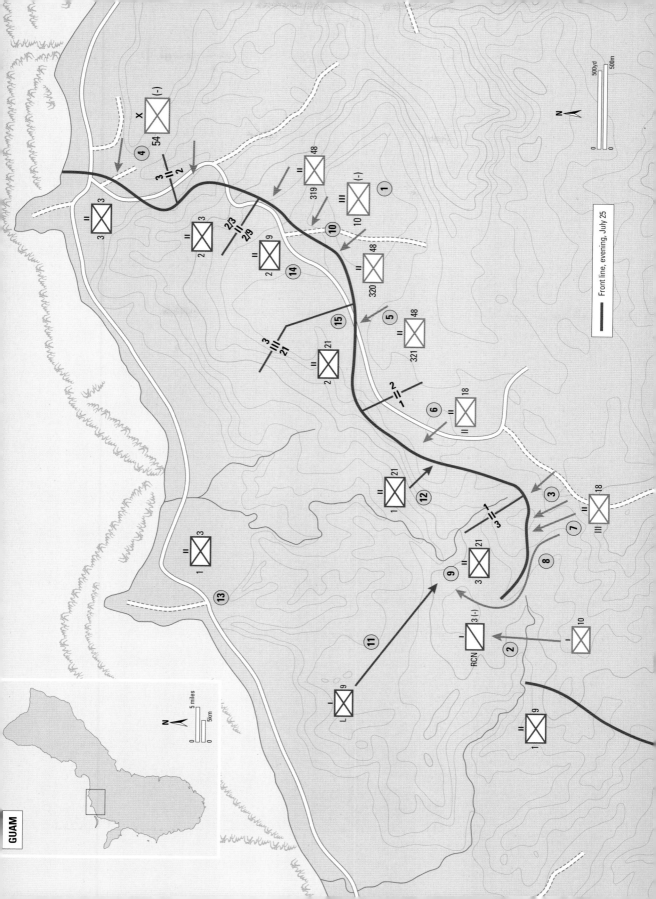

GUAM

N

0   5 miles
0   5km

N

0   500yd
0   500m

Front line, evening, July 25

INTO COMBAT

Marine intelligence had not detected the Japanese preparations for a large counterattack. Some of the infantry in contact with the Japanese defenders had detected and reported anomalous enemy activity during July 24–25, but the first indication that something other than the usual nighttime fighting was in store came at 2330hrs on July 25, when artillery observers reported heavy Japanese activity in the gap between the 21st and 9th Marines. Between then and 0030hrs on July 26, front-line units started reporting Japanese probing. The largest probe was made by a 50-man detachment of the III/18th Infantry against a 25-man detachment of the 3d Marine Division's reconnaissance company deployed in the gap between the 9th and 21st Marines just after midnight. After losing one-third of its men while inflicting 35 casualties, the reconnaissance company withdrew to the 9th Marines' position to its right. At the same time, 15 Japanese launched a bayonet charge against a position manned by elements of the 2/21st Marines; the charge was quickly stopped and all the participants killed.

The timing of the Japanese counterattacks against the 3d Marine Division varied, so they will be described in geographical order along the 3d Marine Division's front. This starts with the 3d Marines on the left (east) side. Then the attacks against the 2/9th Marines (attached to the 3d Marines) are described. Attacks on the 21st Marines' front are described by battalions' sectors, starting with the 2/21st, then the 1/21st, and then the 3/21st Marines. Attacks by infiltration parties in the 3d Marine Division's rear area are addressed lastly.

Before 0100hrs on July 26, the 3d Marines started receiving artillery, mortar, and heavy-machine-gun fire. Artillery and naval-gunfire support were called in to silence this fire. Marines along the perimeter's western and center sections were now reporting fresh probing attacks against their positions. Takashina's counterattack was now underway. In response, US Navy ships begin firing 5in. star shells to light up the ground so Marines could see their enemy; and US Navy fire-control parties with the Marines soon directed 5in and 6in high-explosive shells onto Japanese positions.

On the 3d Marine Division's left, the 54th NGF under Captain (IJN) Sugimoto Yutaka attacked the 3/3d and 2/3d Marines, deployed to the west, during the early hours of July 26. The attack was preceded by intense mortar and artillery fire, including coastal and dual-purpose guns, but this shelling failed to inflict many losses on the well-dug-in Marines. The attack, led by Sugimoto himself, fell apart from the beginning when the 2d Company, 9th Tank Regiment, and 29th Division Tank Company, ordered to support the IJN troops, got lost during the night and failed to locate the rendezvous point. The tanks returned to their hiding places near Ordot and did not participate in the attack. Sugimoto was killed in the initial stages of the attack as Marine riflemen and machine-gunners opened fire from well-prepared positions. Mortar rounds (60mm and 81mm) along with 105mm howitzer shells exploded on the attackers, who fell back. Also killed in the initial fusillade was the executive officer of the 54th NGF. Repeated Japanese attacks during the hours before dawn failed to dent the Marines' lines. Some defenders noted the Japanese charges were uncoordinated and many of the troops involved blundered into Marine fire lanes. Many of the Japanese were sailors of the

217th and 218th Construction battalions and not trained infantrymen. As the sun rose, Japanese survivors retreated toward the hills before Agana.

To the right of the 2/3d Marines was the 2/9th Marines, a battalion that had pushed forward on the lower slopes of the Fonte Plateau during July 25. The 2/9th Marines faced the brunt of the 48th IMB's localized counterattacks as the Japanese tried to retain their starting positions for the planned all-out counterattack. By nightfall the 2/9th Marines held a front of roughly 900yd. Lieutenant Colonel Robert E. Cushman deployed Co. G on his left connecting with the 2/3d Marines, Co. F in the 2/9th Marines' center holding a salient about 150–200yd forward, and Co. E on the right maintaining touch with the 2/21st Marines. Four tanks joined Cushman's battalion at 1825hrs – too late to use in attacks – and were placed in support positions behind the front. US and Japanese front lines were often within hand-grenade range of each other.

During the early evening, localized Japanese counterattacks caused steadily mounting casualties among the US troops. Cushman decided at 2200hrs to pull Co. F, occupying the salient in the battalion's center, back 50yd to align better with its adjacent companies and provide a stronger defensive position. Then, after midnight, the 10th IMR and elements of the 48th IMB launched the first of seven major attacks against the 2/9th Marines. Each charge was repulsed. Although the 2/9th Marines ran low on ammunition and losses mounted, it held its position during the morning hours. The attackers' tactics varied in skill. Some of the Japanese infantry used terrain to approach Marine positions before opening up with all their weapons and resolutely charging with fixed bayonets; these were men of the 10th IMR, which was formed from detachments from the 1st Division, or of the 48th IMB formed from troops of the 11th Division. Other attackers charged across open ground in mass formation. These last men were probably service troops dragooned into infantry service. They served the attack chiefly by drawing US fire.

Marine tanks and infantry advance cautiously along a Guam road, July–August 1944. Once inland from the beaches the US infantry found themselves fighting in jungles and hills. The amphibious nature of the operation became one of supply and support, and combat was similar to any other operation in close terrain. The only difference from fighting on a continent was the availability of naval-gunfire support, ranging from 5in to 16in shells. (USMC 91166)

By dawn the 2/9th Marines was low on ammunition. Riflemen were down to two ammunition clips each, many machine guns were down to their last belt, and mortars had about six rounds per weapon. Just as the Japanese began their last attack, however, the coming of daylight allowed the platoon of M4A2 tanks in the battalion's sector to move to the front and use their 75mm main guns and .50-caliber M2 HMGs to cut up the last Japanese charges. In minutes a second tank platoon arrived escorting ammunition-loaded trucks from the neighboring 3/3d Marines. While the tanks and some riflemen engaged the charging enemy, other Marines quickly unloaded and distributed the much-needed ammunition to their comrades while under fire.

By 0900hrs fighting had subsided on the 2/9th Marines front. With its ammunition replenished and two platoons of tanks in support, the battalion was now ready to renew the fight despite having suffered roughly 50 percent casualties in the preceding 24 hours. The Japanese all-out counterattacking effort was now over after having lost most of their trained infantry. In front of the 2/9th Marines' positions, the bodies of 950 Japanese were found. Later in the campaign, intelligence gathered from Japanese prisoners and captured documents revealed that the IJA's 10th IMR had been reduced to about 100 effectives as a result of its fight against the 2/9th Marines.

To the right of the 2/9th Marines, Lieutenant Colonel Eustace R. Smoak's 2/21st Marines was deployed on a 1,000yd front just north of the Mount Tenjo Road. The battalion had fought its way forward during July 25, suffering many casualties. All rifle and machine-gun units were in the front lines, leaving the battalion without a reserve. Elements of the 48th IMB tested the battalion's defenses, trying to find weak spots through which they could advance into the 3d Marine Division's rear; but the 2/21st Marines' front-line positions held during the night and early-morning hours. Japanese attacks were weak compared to those against neighboring units because the 321st IIB, assigned to this sector, had already suffered heavy losses at the hands of the 2/21st Marines during the day and early evening of July 25.

The 1/21st Marines, under Lieutenant Colonel Marlowe C. Williams, held the center of its regiment's line. Running roughly parallel to the Mount Tenjo Road, the battalion held a front of 1,200yd. This was not a continuous line, however; instead it was a series of squad and platoon strongpoints based on terrain features. Infantry sited their weapons to cover the gaps between positions. Before dark, fire-support controllers registered artillery and naval guns on likely enemy positions and approach routes. The battalion deployed all three of its companies – A, B, and C – in line from east to west.

Throughout the night, Japanese mortar and artillery rounds hit the 1/21st Marines' positions. Then, at about 0400hrs, enemy hand grenades and grenade-discharger rounds exploded in and around the battalion's positions. Following this grenade attack, the IJA's II/18th Infantry (Major Maruyama Chusha) charged, shouting "Wake up American and die!" Some of the charging Japanese passed over the weakened Co. B in the center, which had about 50 men in position.

Once through the battalion's line these Japanese soldiers headed toward the division's rear area. Co. A and Co. C refused their flanks and stood their ground, maintaining steady fire into the charging II/18th Infantry. Machine-

A major consideration for the attack on Guam was that it was US territory. Marines had a long association with Guam since it was taken from Spain during the Spanish–American War of 1898. Here, Marines pose with the plaque from the old Orote Marine Barracks, removed when the Japanese conquered Guam in 1941 and recovered in July 1944. (USMC 88155)

gunners took a heavy toll of some of the attackers, but others were able to silence some US positions with grenades and bayonets. Throughout the attacks, the gunners of the 2/12th Marines provided protective shelling to repulse the enemy. Behind the 1/21st Marines' positions, Co. B, 3d Tank Battalion, had set up positions for the night. These tanks were in the way of the charging Japanese and promptly engaged them with machine guns and 75mm main-gun fire. Japanese climbed onto tanks despite the machine-gun fire and "frantically pounded, kicked, and beat against turrets ... when this seemed futile they leapt to the ground and continued their wild rush down the draw to the rear ..." (Lodge 1954: 81) Despite their losses, some of the attackers reached the positions of the 1/21st Marines' command post and the neighboring 1/21st Marines' 81mm mortar platoons.

Daylight quickly ended the Japanese penetration of the 1/21st Marines' lines. Fire from rifle companies' 60mm mortars made the area where the Japanese had broken through a killing zone and shelled groups of Japanese who were trying to hold their positions. Co. B, 3d Engineer Battalion, and three platoons of the regimental weapons company reinforced the 1/21st Marines. Supported by the tanks of Co. B, 3d Tank Battalion, and naval gunfire, Lieutenant Colonel Williams' battalion counterattacked and regained its front line. The battalion's executive officer, Lieutenant Colonel Ronald R. Van Stockum, subsequently reported that the engineers "advanced as a lead company in at least one of our attacks and performed infantry duties with credit. This is another advantage of basic [infantry] training given to all Marines" (quoted in Shaw, Nalty, & Turnbladh 1966: 512). Japanese infiltrators were tracked down and eliminated by Marine infantry, headquarters, service, and supply troops. By 0800hrs on July 26, the 1/21st Marines restored its lines as of the evening of July 25 and cleared its sector. The IJA's II/18th Infantry was shattered, its commander dead along with almost all other officers.

Both flanks of Lieutenant Colonel Wendell H. Duplantis' 3/21st Marines were unconnected to adjacent units. A small gap separated it from the 1/21st Marines to its left while an 800yd gap separated it from the 9th Marines on its right. All three of the 3/21st Marines' rifle companies – I, L, and K – were deployed in line from east to west. The 3/21st Marines' battalion headquarters was placed on the reverse slope of Hill 460, on the boundary between the 21st and 9th Marines, and in the path of any Japanese attack that tried to exploit the gap between the regiments. Duplantis also positioned a block on a trail in the gap that ran near his battalion's right flank. With all companies on the front line, the battalion's only available reserve was one reinforced rifle squad. Japanese probing attacks started along the 3/21st Marines' front after 0000hrs.

At 0400hrs, while the Japanese II/18th Infantry was attacking 1/21st Marines, its sister battalion, the III/18th Infantry under Major Yukioka Setsuo, launched an assault on the 3/21st Marines. The first Japanese charge gained a temporary advantage when it seized two US machine-gun positions. The Marines quickly recovered these by means of a local counterattack and restored their lines. The III/18th Infantry failed to break the 3/21st Marines' lines; instead, the Japanese moved along the front until they found the gap between the 3/21st Marines' right flank, held by Co. K, and the neighboring 9th Marines. The Japanese quickly advanced into the gap, forcing a platoon outpost of Co. K that was holding the 3/21st Marines' extreme right flank out of its position and back toward the main line. As Major Yukioka's men advanced through the gap, they hit the trail block that Duplantis had placed in the gap. The fighting around Co. K caused Duplantis to commit his sole reserve – one reinforced rifle squad – to cover Co. K's rear. The Japanese strength was such, however, that both the reserve and trail block were overwhelmed.

At Hill 460 the headquarters of the 3/21st Marines soon came under heavy attack; but with front-line troops also under heavy attack, Duplantis decided he could not call on them for help. Headquarters personnel immediately took up their weapons and formed a defense perimeter while the battalion commander informed his superiors that the cipher device was being buried in case the Japanese overran the headquarters. Meanwhile, Major Yukioka deployed his men on the high ground between Co. K and the 3/21st Marines' headquarters. Machine-gun fire was directed into the rear of Co. K and grenade dischargers and mortars targeted the headquarters. These positions remained static as both sides exchanged fire. As daylight broke, however, the Marines prepared a counterattack to restore their lines. Co. L, 9th Marines, supported by machine-gun fire from Co. B, 9th Marines, and artillery, drove Japanese troops from their positions in the gap and around Co. K and the 3/21st Marines' headquarters. Many of the Japanese trying to escape Co. L's drive blundered into waiting Marines of the 3/21st Marines' front line and were killed; others fled north before the 21st and 9th Marines closed the gap that had separated the two regiments the night before.

After the Japanese attacks against his regiment started, Colonel Arthur H. Butler, the commander of the 21st Marines, organized a regimental reserve line under his executive officer, Lieutenant Colonel Ernest W. Fry, Jr. This line was established on high ground overlooking the beach and was formed from elements of Co. E, 19th Marines (Pioneers), the 21st Marines' H&S company, elements of 3d Motor Transport Battalion, and a few men of the 2/12th Marines (Artillery). Some Japanese soldiers that had moved through the gap between the 21st and 9th Marines had already advanced, however. Among them were demolition parties tasked with destroying US artillery pieces and supply dumps; but many of these Japanese ended up near the 3d Marine Division's hospital area at about 0630hrs. Two companies of Pioneers were quickly dispatched to the scene. Before the Pioneers arrived, however, 41 wounded Marines grabbed any available weapons and, together with doctors and corpsmen, formed a defense of the hospital as the more seriously wounded men were evacuated to the beach. This improvised detachment held that Japanese at bay until the Pioneers could clear the area. Other Japanese reached the artillery positions, but were killed by men of the 12th Marines.

By noon on July 26, the 3d Marine Division's lines had been restored and the Japanese counterattack was over. The 3d Marine Division suffered 166 dead, 645 wounded, and 34 missing. Japanese losses totaled around 3,500. IIIAC's daily report summarized the Japanese attack:

Enemy attack began Tuesday AM, increased considerably during the evening and throughout the night. This attack was supported by intense artillery and mortar fire. By daylight enemy forces of considerable strength had infiltrated the beachhead. These enemy units attacked down hill by rolling charges with special attempts at emplaced artillery. Later attacks unsuccessful. Captured document indicates this was coordinated all-out attack by at least 6 Bns to drive Division from ASAN beach head. At dawn all units of 3RD MARDIV, including Pioneers, and Hqs Bn began clearing Beachhead … Many hundreds … killed within and outside of lines. Our front lines intact at conclusion of this period. (III Amphibious Corps, September 3, 1944: 445)

ABOVE LEFT
Men of the 3d Marine Division view the bodies of Japanese troops of the 48th IMB and 29th Infantry Division, killed on the Fonte Ridge during the night of July 25/26, 1944. During this night the Japanese launched a well-planned counterattack using most of their infantry in an attempt to overrun the Marines' beachhead and drive them back into the sea. This attack failed at the cost of most of the IJA's infantry leadership and rank and file on Guam. (INP/Bettmann Archive/Getty Images)

ABOVE RIGHT
After the failed counterattack on July 25/26, 1944, Japanese morale on Guam started to crack. Some Japanese began to surrender, more than Marines had seen in prior battles. Here two Marines help a Japanese combatant out of his dugout to surrender. These Marines are wearing elements of the old 1942 camouflage uniform that had been largely replaced by the sage-green uniform. (USMC 88071)

Peleliu

September 15–21, 1944

BACKGROUND TO BATTLE

Peleliu Island lies some 840nmi southwest of Guam and 600nmi due east of Davao City in the Philippines. The 1st Marine Division assaulted Peleliu on September 15, 1944. Before the attack, the divisional commander, Major General William H. Rupertus, told subordinates that he "expected the operation to be very tough but very short, comparable to Tarawa" (quoted in Hough 1950: 35). Peleliu was a very tough fight, and it lasted far longer than that for Tarawa Atoll, Japanese resistance continuing until November 27. By then, the 1st Marine Division had been relieved by the US Army's 81st Infantry Division.

Earlier 1st Marine Division battles (Guadalcanal and Cape Gloucester) had involved unopposed landings followed by weeks or months of jungle fighting. Peleliu became the 1st Marine Division's first assault across coral reefs while under fire. As the division prepared to assault Peleliu, approximately 30 percent of its men had been in the Pacific for at least 24 months and were veterans of the fighting on Guadalcanal and Cape Gloucester; another 30 percent had 12 months' overseas service including Cape Gloucester; and the remaining 40 percent were fresh replacements. Experienced in jungle warfare, the division expected victory in its next fight against the Japanese.

On Peleliu, the Japanese changed their island-defense policy. With no intervention by the Combined Fleet planned, and given the past failures of counterattacks to destroy enemy beachheads, the Japanese High Command realized that isolated islands would be lost. Island defenders, such as Peleliu's, were now ordered to deny US forces use of their island, especially airfields, for as long as possible and inflict as many US casualties as they could. Defenses were now built in depth and located to minimize destruction during the

intense pre-invasion bombardment that had become synonymous with US amphibious assaults. Counterattacks were to be planned and executed carefully. Peleliu's defenders put these orders into effect so that by September 15, when the 1st Marine Division attacked, the battle for the island would be unlike any encountered to date.

On Peleliu, minefields were laid on beaches and frequently extended up to 100yd inland. Offshore, obstacles were built to channel landing craft into passages that artillery and mortars were preregistered to fire upon. Antitank ditches and barriers were dug and heavy strands of barbed wire strung behind possible landing beaches. Artillery and mortars were emplaced on the Umurbrogol Ridge and smaller coral outcroppings and sited to fire on the airfield, beaches, and low areas. Natural and manmade cover was expertly used to hide many defensive positions from the US forces. This was especially true of the Umurbrogol Ridge, where extensive jungle growth hid many fortifications from US aerial observation and photography; frequently, positions were not discovered until shelling had destroyed the vegetation and they were spotted by advancing riflemen. Detailed counterattack plans were made and rehearsed. The Japanese even used pre-invasion US air raids to train troops to maneuver under live fire. Several infantry companies were reorganized into specialized counterattack units that abandoned conventional platoon organization. Teams of two or three men were trained to conduct demolitions attacks against US tanks. If US troops established a firm beachhead, the Japanese planned to withdraw to positions on the Umurbrogol Ridge.

Defending Peleliu was the reinforced 2d Infantry Regiment of the 14th Division, commanded by Colonel Nakagawa Kunio. Attached to the 2d Infantry Regiment were the III/15th Infantry, the 346th IIB of the 53d IMB, and the 14th Division tank unit (12 tanks). IJN units on Peleliu included a detachment of the 45th NGF, the 114th and 126th AAA units, the 204th and 214th Construction battalions, and stranded aviation personnel. During the battle the II/15th Infantry was moved to Peleliu using the 14th Division's sea-transport capability. Colonel Nakagawa placed his I/2d Infantry in reserve and divided the island into four battalion

ABOVE LEFT
Peleliu being shelled during the pre-invasion bombardment, conducted during September 12–15, 1944. Looking to the northeast, this photograph was taken from a spotter plane from the light cruiser USS *Honolulu* (CL-48). The airfield is in the foreground and the Umurbrogol Ridge, partly shrouded in smoke, is in the distance. (USN 80-G-283520)

ABOVE RIGHT
The first assault waves advance toward the beach at Peleliu, September 15, 1944. In the foreground are LVTs while LVT(A)s are the first wave closer to the island. Vessels closer to the beach are LCI(G)s and landing control craft. Peleliu is in the midst of being shelled and bombed, as shown by the explosions and rising smoke. (US Navy/Interim Archives/Getty Images)

Lewis Burwell "Chesty" Puller remains the most decorated Marine in US history. He was awarded five Navy Crosses and one Distinguished Service Cross; the Medal of Honor is the only higher US decoration. A distant cousin of the US Army's General George S. Patton, Puller was born on June 26, 1898. He began his 37-year US Marine Corps career as a private, enlisting in August 1918 after leaving the Virginia Military Institute in Lexington. After basic training he attended the noncommissioned officers' school and Officer Candidate School at Quantico, Virginia, and was commissioned second lieutenant in the Marine Reserves on June 16, 1919. Post-1918 reductions in the size of the US Marine Corps resulted in Puller being put on inactive status ten days later and given the active rank of corporal. He served as a Marine NCO and as an acting officer in the Haitian Gendarmerie between 1919 and 1921. He was recommissioned as a second lieutenant on March 6, 1924. In December 1928 he was assigned to the US Marine Corps detachment assisting the Nicaraguan National Guard during the US intervention. In both Haiti and Nicaragua he saw extensive small-unit combat and jungle warfare.

Puller served as the battalion commander of the 1/7th Marines in the 1st Marine Division on Guadalcanal. Later he became the executive officer of the 7th Marines and served in that position during the Cape Gloucester operation on New Britain Island. He was promoted to colonel on February 1, 1944, and assigned to command the 1st Marines, leading the regiment during the battle of Peleliu. He again commanded the 1st Marines during the Korean War (1950–53), leading the regiment at Incheon and the Chosin Reservoir. Promoted to brigadier general in January 1951, he then served as the 1st Marine Division's assistant division commander in Korea. He was also the acting division commander during February and March that year. After suffering a stroke, Puller retired from the US Marine Corps in 1955 with the rank of lieutenant general. He resided in Virginia until his death on October 11, 1971.

OPPOSITE
Marine riflemen moving along a beach on Peleliu with an LVT(A)-4 behind them. While this appears to be a posed photograph, it does show the physical condition of the sandy beaches on Peleliu, Note the Marines with full combat gear and packs, and the unique profile of the 75mm M2 howitzer-armed LVT(A)-4. (PhotoQuest/Getty Images)

sectors, giving the 346th IIB the northwestern, the II/2d Infantry the northeastern, the III/15th Infantry the southeastern, and the III/2d Infantry the southwestern sector. The 2d Infantry Regiment's artillery battalion manned four 75mm Type 95 field guns and four 105mm Type 91 howitzers. A provisional heavy mortar unit was present with four 150mm mortars. The III/15th Infantry included an artillery company with four 75mm guns and a mortar company with ten 81mm mortars. The US Marine Corps subsequently estimated Japanese strength to have included about 5,300 IJA troops, 800–1,000 IJN combatants, and more than 4,000 naval-construction and airbase personnel.

The 1st Marine Division landed on the southwestern beaches of Peleliu on September 15, 1944; the regiments involved in the landings were (north to south) the 1st Marines, 5th Marines, and 7th Marines. Except for the southernmost beach, these sectors were defended by the IJA's III/2d Infantry. The 1st Marine Division's assignment was to advance inland, pivot on its left and seize the Umurbrogol Ridge. On D-Day, the 3/1st Marines landed on Beach White 1 and the 2/1st Marines on Beach White 2; the 1/1st Marines formed the regimental reserve. LVT(A)s and LVTs approached Peleliu uneventfully until the leading waves crossed the line of departure, at which point Japanese artillery and mortars began targeting the vehicles. This Japanese barrage moved with the leading waves, increasing in volume as the vehicles approached the beaches. Antiboat, antitank, and heavy machine guns opened fire from enfilade positions when the US first wave was 50–100yd offshore. The first LVT(A)s reached the beach at about 0830hrs and moved inland, quickly followed by LVTs carrying US Marine Corps infantry. Most of the LVTs were halted near the beach by tangled undergrowth immediately inland.

Nakagawa Kunio

Colonel Nakagawa Kunio was the commander of the IJA's 2d Infantry Regiment and in charge of the Japanese defense of Peleliu, although Major General Murai Kenjiro was present in order to offset the presence of the IJN's Vice Admiral Ito Yoshioka. Nakagawa was born on January 23, 1898, the son of an elementary-school principal. In December 1918 he graduated in the 30th class of the IJA Academy, was commissioned a second lieutenant, and assigned to the 48th Infantry Regiment. He subsequently served in the 12th Division's headquarters and commanded a battalion of the 79th Infantry Regiment. His first experience of combat was during the Marco Polo Bridge Incident (July 7–9, 1937) that marked the beginning of the Second Sino-Japanese War (1937–45). He served in China until March 1939 when he was ordered to the IJA Staff College and promoted to lieutenant colonel following the recommendation of his regimental commander. Four years later he was promoted to colonel and assigned to command the 2d Infantry Regiment, which was part of the 14th Division stationed in Manchuria as part of the Kwantung Army.

As US forces advanced in the Central Pacific, the 14th Division was sent to help defend the Japanese-held Palau Islands. Once there, the 2d Infantry Regiment was assigned to Peleliu, lying south of the main islands in the Palau group. Unlike some other Japanese officers, Nakagawa embraced the new doctrine of protracted island defense. Although orders and announcements to his troops continued to mention destroying the enemy on the beaches, he skillfully exploited the natural strength of Peleliu and manmade fortifications and connecting tunnels to mount a prolonged defense in depth that lasted until November 24, 1944, when, acknowledging that the battle was lost, he committed ritual suicide. On December 31, 1944, Nagakawa was posthumously promoted to the rank of lieutenant general in the IJA.

MAP KEY

1 0831hrs, September 15: Co. K, 1st Marines lands on Beach White 1. It reorganizes and attacks the Point.

2 0930hrs, September 15: By this time, the 2/1st Marines has advanced through heavy woods against moderate resistance and reached about 350yd inland.

3 1020hrs, September 15: Co. K, 1st Marines captures the Point and is soon isolated from the rest of the 1st Marine Division for the next 30 hours.

4 c.1700hrs, September 15: The 1st Marine Division establishes a defense line for the night.

5 0800hrs, September 16: The 1st Marine Regiment attacks and heads north, toward the Umurbrogol Mountain.

6 1530hrs, September 16: After heavy fighting, elements of the 1/1st and 3/1st Marines make contact with Co. K, 1st Marines at the Point.

7 c.1700hrs, September 16: The 2/1st Marines reaches the northern edge of the built-up area and digs in for the night.

8 c.2200hrs, September 16: Approximately 500 Japanese mount a frontal attack on the Point. By 0200hrs on September 17, Co. K has shattered the Japanese attack.

9 0600hrs, September 17: The 1st Marines prepares to renew its attack. Having suffered over 1,000 casualties over two days, all three battalions are needed on the front line; the 3/1st Marines on the left next to the shore, the 1/1st Marines in the center, and the 2/1st Marines on the right. The 2/7th Marines is placed under the command of the 1st Marines as its reserve.

10 0845hrs, September 17: The 2/1st Marines advances slowly against heavy Japanese resistance.

11 0900hrs, September 17: Supported by tanks, artillery, and naval gunfire, the 1/1st Marines reduces Japanese pillboxes on its front and advances through thick jungle to the O-1 line.

12 1155hrs, September 17: The 2/1st Marines continues to attack into the Umurbrogol foothills, reorganizing under fire to maintain combat effectiveness.

13 c.1700hrs, September 17: The 1/1st Marines holds the forward slopes on the first series of hills and pinnacles of the Umurbrogol Ridge; the 2/1st Marines controls the crest of Hill 200.

14 0700hrs, September 18: After a 30-minute air, naval gunfire, and artillery preparation, the 3/1st, 2/7th, and 2/1st Marines launch a coordinated attack. The 2/1st and 2/7th Marines capture Hill 210 after heavy fighting.

15 1630hrs, September 18: The 2/1st Marines captures Hill 205, but finds that it does not connect with the main ridge system. The 1st Marines has now reached the southern face of what will become the final Japanese pocket of resistance on Peleliu.

16 September 21: After attacking the Umurbrogol Mountain during September 16–21 while elements of the 5th and 7th Marines secure the southern and eastern parts of Peleliu, the 1st Marines is relieved. After losing over 50 percent of its strength, the regiment's fight on Peleliu is over. Peleliu is declared secured by the US Army's 81st Infantry Division on November 27.

Battlefield environment

Peleliu Island has an area of 6.56 square miles and is surrounded by mangrove swamp covering over one-quarter of its area. Located 7 degrees north of the equator, the island has a tropical rainforest climate. Rain is heavy throughout the year and averages 160in annually. During September and October the daily temperatures can be as high as 88°F with a relative humidity of 82 percent, resulting in a heat index of 108°F, classified as dangerous to humans. Once part of the ocean's floor and covered with coral, Peleliu was formed when underground volcanic action forced the ocean floor above the sea surface. Parts of the island remained visually similar to natural coral that can be seen on any tropical reef. The Umurbrogol Ridge was formed where the subterranean pressure was greatest. This pressure raised, buckled, and cracked the sea bed and coral as they rose. This action formed ridges and valleys covered with rubble, jagged boulders, steep slopes, and sheer cliffs. The 1st Marines' regimental report described the terrain of the Umurbrogol Ridge as:

... the worst ever encountered by the regiment in three Pacific campaigns. Along its center, the rocky spine was heaved up in a contorted mass of decayed coral, strewn with rubble, crags, ridges and gulches thrown together in a confusing maze. There were no roads, scarcely any trails. The pock-marked surface offered no secure footing even in the few level places. It was impossible to dig in: the best the men could do was pile a little coral or wood debris around their positions. The jagged rock slashed their shoes and clothes, and tore their bodies every time they hit the deck for safety. Casualties were higher for the simple reason it was impossible to get under the ground away from the Japanese mortar barrages. Each blast hurled chunks of coral in all directions, multiplying many times the fragmentation effect of every shell. (Quoted in Hough 1950: 77)

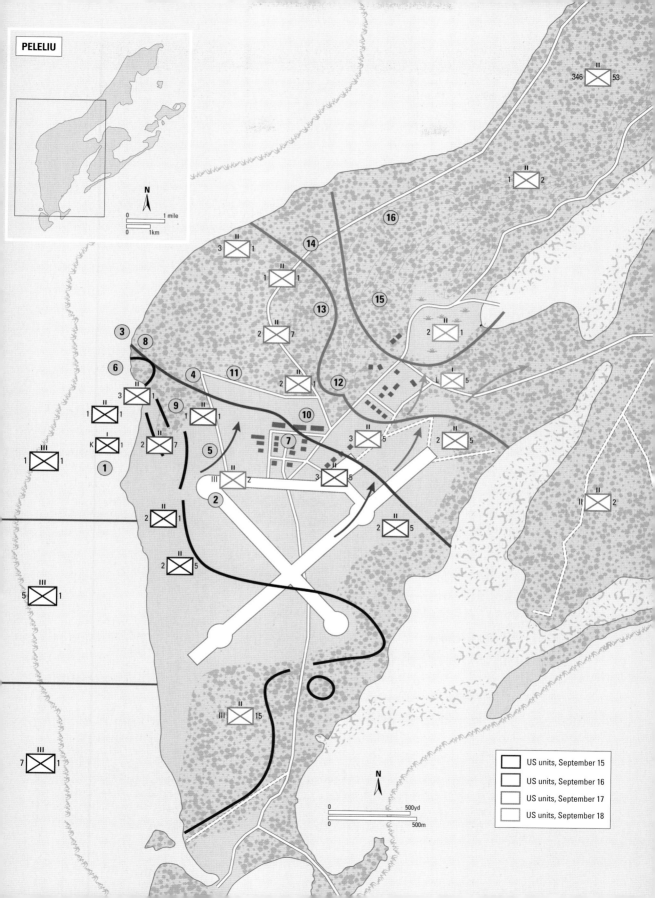

PELELIU

N

0   1 mile
0   1km

346 | 53

1 | 2

3 | 1

16

14

1 | 1

2 | 7

13

15

2 | 1

3

8

2 | 1

6

4

11

12

2 | 1

3 | 1

3 | 1

9

2 | 7

2 | 1

1 | 1

10

5

7

K | 1

3 | 5

2 | 5

2 | 5

1 | 1

III | 2

3 | 5

II | 2

2

2 | 1

2 | 5

5 | 1

2 | 5

7 | 1

III | 15

N

0   500yd
0   500m

US units, September 15
US units, September 16
US units, September 17
US units, September 18

INTO COMBAT

The attackers' left battalion, the 3/1st Marines, met heavy Japanese flanking fire from the Point, a jagged coral outcropping jutting into the sea and rising about 30ft above the water just beyond Beach White 1's northern boundary. From it a Japanese 47mm gun and machine guns fired along Beach White 1. This fire and the current off Peleliu caused the LVTs carrying Co. K (the 1st Marine Division's northernmost unit) to land 100yd south of their intended position at 0831hrs. At 0834hrs, the battalion commander, Lieutenant Colonel Stephen V. Sabol, and his advance command post landed and moved 50yd inland. At 0844hrs, Co. L (in reserve) completed landing while Co. I had advanced about 150yd inland and encountered a steep, long, and rugged coral ridge 30ft high, fortified by the Japanese using natural caves and manmade positions. This ridge was not on any maps and had not been identified in US aerial reconnaissance photographs. Co. I suffered 15 percent casualties and needed to reorganize. Co. K, on the left, advanced toward the Point against heavy fire.

The sixth wave landed at 0849hrs with the remainder of the battalion command post and its 81mm mortar platoon, but these were soon pinned down. On the 3/1st Marines' right, the 2/1st Marines under Lieutenant Colonel Russell E. Honsowetz landed on Beach White 2. The 2/1st Marines advanced inland through dense woods encountering moderate resistance. Supported by LVT(A)s and M4A2 tanks, Honsowetz's battalion reached the O-1 phase line roughly 350yd inland at about 0930hrs. Having made contact with the 1/5th Marines on its right, the 2/1st Marines was ordered to hold its position until further notice because the 3/1st Marines, on its left, had been halted.

At 0915hrs, Co. I resumed its advance. Slowed by swampy ground and heavy enemy fire, it stalled in front of the coral ridge and lost contact with Co. K on its left. Elements of Co. L, the battalion reserve, were committed to establish contact between Co. K and Co. I, but were pinned down by Japanese fire from the coral ridge facing Co. I. Another Co. L platoon tried

D-day on Peleliu, September 15, 1944. Within minutes of its first waves landing, the 1st Marine Regiment would find itself confronting well-dug-in Japanese soldiers. Just inland was this coral ridge, which was honeycombed with Japanese infantry fighting positions including machine guns. Having suffered heavy casualties, US forces were not able to secure this position until the following day. (USMC 2-10 21508904022)

to contact Co. K, but it too became embroiled in the fight before the coral ridge. At 1145hrs Co. A, 1st Marines, was attached to the 3/1st Marines to close the gap with Co. K. Co. A was unable to contact Co. K, however, and suffered heavy losses. Co. B was committed at 1415hrs, but suffered the same fate. By nightfall, troops of the 1/1st Marines and Co. I and Co. L of the 3/1st Marines had dug in without having made contact with Co. K.

Commanded by Captain George P. Hunt, Co. K's mission was to capture the Point and secure the 1st Marine Division's left flank. Hunt, a US Marine Corps reservist and prewar journalist, subsequently described the Point as a mass of solid jagged coral, full of crevasses, boulders, and sharp upcroppings with a near-perpendicular wall facing the beach. In the wall, the Japanese had built five steel-and-concrete pillboxes; one contained a 47mm gun and the others HMGs. Between six and 12 Japanese were stationed in each pillbox. On top of the coral wall were positions manned by personnel from the III/2d Infantry. The 3/1st Marines' report described the advance against the Point:

Just a short distance inland from the beach at Peleliu, Marines encountered coral ridges. Their sometimes near-vertical sides covered with thick jungle vegetation made climbing difficult. Added to this was the frequent presence of Japanese troops concealed in hidden positions who could suddenly open fire on exposed Marines. Peleliu quickly became a hell on earth for Marine riflemen. (NARA N-95463)

Company K had initiated its turning movement to the north as originally planned. The 3rd platoon on the left had fought to within 50 yards of the point clearing the beach of one 40mm gun, two heavy machine guns, and numerous light machine guns. The 2nd platoon on the right had advanced inland 75 yards through rifle and machine gun fire to a tank trap where it was pinned down by extremely heavy fire from a coral ridge about 30 to 40 feet high to its front. At this time the two platoons each had the equivalent of about one squad left. In the 3rd platoon, the platoon leader, platoon sergeant, and guide were casualties; and in the second platoon leader and platoon sergeant were also casualties. Due to these casualties and the excessive front a large gap developed between the two platoons and the Battalion CP was so informed. Due to the tactical advantage of the point the first platoon was committed in the third platoon's sector with the mission of securing the point ... (3/1 Report 1944: 4)

Before 1015hrs, 1st and 3d Platoons of Co. K stormed the Point. With their protecting infantry eliminated, the five Japanese pillboxes were attacked from blind spots and reduced by 1020hrs. Co. K, however, was now isolated. For the next 30 hours, resupply and the evacuation of wounded Marines was conducted by LVTs that shuttled between Beach White 1 and the Point. At one time during the first night only 18 Marines with a captured Japanese HMG held the Point. By holding the Point, Co. K allowed the 1st Marine Division to consolidate the beachhead. The division's beachhead was approximately 300yd inland of the northern beaches, curving inland about 1,400yd in the center, and curved back toward the southernmost beach.

On D+1 (September 16), a heavy naval and air bombardment prepared the way for the Marines' attack. It was a hot day, and the high temperature of 105°F caused many heat prostration cases. The 1st Marines' attack started at 0800hrs, pivoting north while keeping in contact with the 5th Marines. The first goal was to establish contact with Co. K on the Point and secure the coral ridge that had stopped the rest of the 3/1st Marines on D-day. Supported by two M4A2s tanks, Co. L attacked the coral ridge and, after about one hour of heavy fighting, captured its southern end. After reorganizing, Co. L advanced along the coral ridge's top, taking its defenders in the flank. Co. B followed Co. L and mopped up bypassed Japanese defenders. Progress was slow and losses mounted. Co. C was inserted left of Co. L at about 1100hrs to try to close the gap with Co. K. At about 1430hrs, Co. L and Co. B attacked along the ridge northwesterly toward the Point. At 1530hrs, elements of Co. B made contact with Co. K; the latter company then advanced about 100yd to strengthen its line.

At about 1700hrs, Marines started preparing night defense positions against an expected Japanese counterattack. The 3/1st Marines' line was now composed, left to right, of Co. K holding the Point, then Co. C, then the rest of Co. B (which relieved Co. L when it pulled back to reorganize), and finally Co. I, which connected with the 2/1st Marines. Personnel of the 1/1st and 3/1st Marines were intermixed under command of the 3/1st Marines. The final act of the day occurred at about 2200hrs, when roughly 500 Japanese made a frontal attack on the Point and along the coast. Co. K, supported by flanking fire from Co. B and Co. C, shattered the Japanese attack by 0200hrs D+2 (September 17). By that time, Co. K had 78 remaining out of 235 men landed on D-day. Marines found bodies at the Point and the coral ridge with identity markers from the 3d, 7th, and 9th companies of the IJA's 2d Infantry Regiment.

On the 3/1st Marines' right, the 2/1st Marines attacked at 0800hrs with Co. E and Co. F in line. In 15 minutes, Co. F reported crossing the airfield's western turning circle under heavy fire. At 0829hrs, Co. F entered the building area and engaged Japanese forces that were using damaged reinforced-concrete buildings as fighting positions. Marines had to clear each structure one at a time. By day's end, the 2/1st Marines had advanced into the northern portion of the building area where the battalion prepared defenses for the night. The 1st Marines' experiences at the Point and coral ridge on D-day and D+1 were a precursor to those on the Umurbrogol Ridge: "All the trials which the 1st Marines had suffered up to this point were compounded by the protracted hell which commenced for the regiment on D-plus 2" (Hough 1950: 77).

On D+2 the 1st Marines renewed the attack. First, the regiment reorganized and returned its intermixed rifle companies, platoons, and squads to their parent battalions. Colonel Lewis B. "Chesty" Puller's regiment had suffered more than 1,000 casualties during two days ashore. These losses meant that all three battalions were needed on the front line for the September 17 attack: the 3/1st Marines on the left next to the shore; the 1/1st Marines in the center; and the 2/1st Marines on the right and connecting with the 5th Marines. The 2/7th Marines, division reserve, which had not landed on D-day, was placed under the 1st Marines in reserve and its Co. E moved up in close support of the 2/1st Marines.

African American troops of either the 16th Field Depot USMC or the 17th Special Naval Construction Battalion USN on the beach at Peleliu, September 15, 1944. Both of these units were assigned to the shore party supporting the 1st Marine Division. The men of these units carried supplies to the front lines and then returned carrying wounded. African American Marines and sailors fought alongside white Marines on multiple occasions, and both units received commendations for their actions on Peleliu. (Archive Photos/Getty Images)

On the 1st Marines' left, Lieutenant Colonel Sabol's 3/1st Marines had a relatively easy day. The battalion's sector was the coastal flat land that bordered the Umurbrogol Ridge's coral massif to the right. Facing resistance from elements of the III/2d Infantry, the US battalion advanced 700yd behind a curtain of heavy fire from ships, artillery, and air bombardment. The battalion stopped its advance when the 1/1st Marines, on its right, was held up by heavy Japanese resistance, and prepared positions for the night. Co. K was in the center on higher ground with swampy ground separating it from Co. I (on the left) and Co. L (on the right). These gaps were covered by fire from 60mm and 81mm mortars and prearranged artillery barrages in case of a Japanese attack. The 3/1st Marines lost 59 men this day.

In the regiment's center was the 1/1st Marines under Major Raymond G. Davis. D+2 was the first day on Peleliu that the 1/1st Marines was employed as a battalion instead of having its companies parceled out to other battalions. Almost immediately, however, the 3d Platoon of Co. B, with a machine-gun squad, was attached to Co. L of the 3/1st Marines. Co. B's 1st Platoon and 2d Platoon were attached to Co. A and Co. C respectively. Co. B was re-formed around 1700hrs under its acting commander, Lieutenant Francis D. Rineer. In the 1/1st Marines' center was a defensive position consisting of a large concrete blockhouse with 4ft-thick walls and connected by tunnels with 12 surrounding concrete-and-coral pillboxes. These fortifications had escaped the pre-invasion naval bombardment, but had been identified the previous day by US patrols. Before the 1/1st Marines attacked, its naval fire-support control team directed shelling by the 14in guns of one of the battleships – variously reported as USS *Idaho* (BB-42), USS *Mississippi* (BB-41), or USS *Pennsylvania* (BB-38) – against this complex. Armor-piercing and high-capacity shells shattered the Japanese blockhouse.

At 0900hrs, Co. C, on the left and in contact with the 3/1st Marines, and Co. A on the right, jumped off. Supported by tanks, artillery, and naval gunfire, the 1/1st Marines soon reduced the Japanese pillboxes and then advanced through thick jungle to the O-1 line. This advance extended the battalion's front and the 1st and 2d Platoons of Co. B were attached to Co. A and Co. C respectively. After a short pause to reorganize, the 1/1st Marines resumed its advance toward the O-2 line. The battalion now entered the foothills of the Umurbrogol Ridge. The Japanese were hitting the battalion with heavy rifle, machine-gun, mortar, and artillery fire from higher ground, causing heavy casualties. Until now, the 1/1st Marines had only identified the IJA's 2d Infantry Regiment, but as Co. A started forward, the 45th NGF made an appearance: "a heavy machine gun squad with the insignia of the Imperial ... Marines on their caps began to set up in the rear of the platoons' position; several of the men noticed the situation and automatic weapons, carbines, and M-1's opened fire killing all the ... Marines but one" (1/1 Report 1944: 15).

The 1/1st Marines moved forward and stormed the high ground known as Hill 200, a 200ft ridge that made a salient in the battalion's center as Marines advanced on the lower ground to its sides. Hill 200 had steep sides, sometimes nearly vertical, which were honeycombed with caves containing Japanese defenses. Marines had to claw their way up vertiginous coral ridges and then climb down into steep ravines while trying to shelter from enemy fire. US riflemen, aided by tanks when possible, used bazookas and eliminated 35 Japanese cave positions. By day's end, the 1/1st Marines held the forward slopes of the first series of hills and pinnacles of the Umurbrogol Ridge. The battalion had captured or destroyed 37 Japanese pillboxes plus two 47mm, two 70mm, and one naval 6in gun. It counted over 300 Japanese dead.

On the right, the 2/1st Marines attacked at 0820hrs, overrunning the road that marked the O-2 line. At 0845hrs, Co. E reported advancing slowly due to resistance and had destroyed three pillboxes. Two minutes later, Co. G reached the base of the Umurbrogol Ridge and the 2/1st Marines had advanced 150yd beyond the O-2 line. Heavy fire came from Hill 200, from where Japanese observers directed mortar and artillery fire against Marines below, including the neighboring 5th Marines to the 1st Marines' right. To eliminate this shelling, the 2/1st Marines was ordered to assault Hill 200.

While attacking up the steep sides of Hill 200, Marines suffered heavy casualties. Japanese mortars and machine guns maintained a near-continuous fire from the hill and adjacent positions. The crews of mountain guns and dual-purpose artillery pieces emerged from caves, fired their guns, and quickly disappeared back into their hiding positions. US casualties increased quickly and many of the M4A2s and LVT(A)s supporting the 2/1st Marines were put out of action by Japanese fire. At 1155hrs, Co. G reported that it had suffered 87 casualties since 0800hrs. The assault continued and units reorganized under fire to maintain combat effectiveness. By nightfall, the 2/1st Marines controlled the crest of Hill 200. The Japanese brought heavy fire to bear on the captured position from Hill 210 to the west. Marines struggled to construct defensive positions in the coral: "The impossibility of 'digging in' in any accepted sense of that term cannot be over-emphasized if a true picture of the fighting on Peleliu is to be given. Repeatedly it was the controlling factor in nullifying costly gains" (Hough 1950: 90).

In the 2/1st Marines' sector, the Americans held a deep salient jutting into the Japanese line along the crest of Hill 200. The parallel ridge to its west was in Japanese hands and formed a deep salient in the US lines. After dusk a gap was created between the 2/1st and 1/1st Marines when lines were adjusted for the night. Co. F, 7th Marines, attacked into this gap and closed it. To help defend Hill 200 during the night, Co. G, 7th Marines, was brought up at 0200hrs on September 18 and attached to the 2/1st Marines.

From D-day through D+2, the 1st Marines suffered 1,236 casualties out of an initial strength of 3,218. To replace infantry losses, the regiment put every available man in the front line and received 115 men from the 1st Pioneer Battalion as

Soldiers of the US Army's 81st Infantry Division climb one of the steep slopes of the Umurbrogol Ridge on Peleliu. Marines faced the same type of terrain while serving on the island. The 81st Infantry Division relieved the 1st Marine Division after the latter had suffered heavy casualties and remained on Peleliu until February 1945, carrying out mopping-up actions around the Palau Islands. These were the 81st Infantry Division's only major combat operations. (Photoquest/Getty Images)

replacements. On the morning of September 18, the 3/1st Marines started with a total of 473 effectives, 200 of whom were from the regiment's headquarters. At 0600hrs, the 2/7th Marines, under Lieutenant Colonel Spencer S. Berger, replaced the 1/1st Marines, which became the regiment's reserve. A 30-minute air, naval gunfire, and artillery preparation began at 0630hrs. Then at 0700hrs, the 3/1st, 2/7th, and 2/1st Marines started their attack. Hill 210 was captured after savage and costly fighting by the 2/1st and 2/7th Marines. The Japanese responded with strong counterattacks against elements of the 2/1st Marines located on Hill 200 that forced the Marines back. At 1400hrs, Lieutenant Colonel Honsowetz reported his troops' situation was desperate and requested a smoke barrage and reinforcements. Co. B from the 1/1st Marines was attached to the 2/1st Marines, and assaulted Hill 205, which lay forward and to the right of Hill 200. Co. B captured this hill by 1630hrs, but found it did not connect with the main ridge system. Continuing its attack, Co. B found itself amid a complex of sharp peaks, gullies, and ridges that stopped its advance. Co. B had reached the southern face of the final Japanese pocket of resistance on Peleliu. On the 1st Marines' left, the 3/1st Marines met little opposition, but had to restrict its forward advance to a few hundred yards to keep in contact with the 2/7th Marines attacking on the Umurbrogol Ridge.

The 1st Marines continued fighting on Peleliu until September 21, D+6. By that date, casualties totaled 1,749, or 56 percent. The 1/1st Marines lost 71 percent, the 2/1st Marines lost 56 percent, the 3/1st Marines lost 55 percent, and the regimental headquarters and weapons companies lost 32 percent. At this point the 1/1st Marines' nine rifle platoons totaled 74 men, including replacements, and none of the original platoon leaders remained. Peleliu was a tough fight, and one unlike the regiment's previous battles.

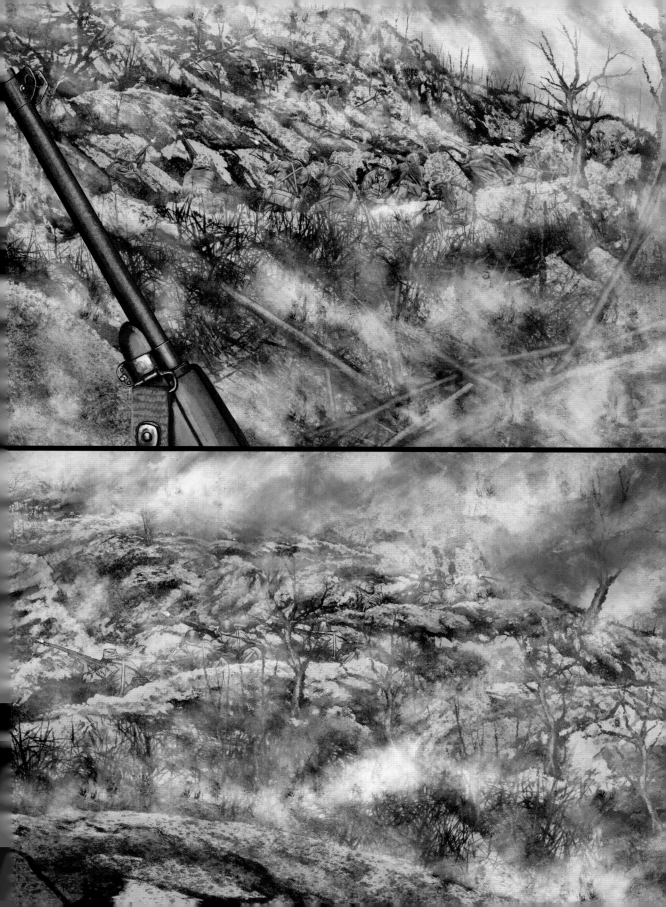

Contesting Hill 200

US view: On D+2, September 17, 1944, the 2/1st Marines attacked Hill 200, defended by elements of the IJA's 2nd Infantry Regiment. A Marine officer, using a coral outcropping as cover, is looking north along the rising slope of the eastern side of Hill 200. In front of him is the jagged Umurbrogol Mountain, with shells exploding and smoke rising from the ongoing bombardment of Japanese positions along the ridges. To his immediate left is his radio man with a backpacked SCR-300 FM radio. Ahead and to the right are two BAR teams, seven riflemen, a bazooka team, and one squad leader. To the immediate left is an M1919A4 LMG team. Farther to the left are a BAR team and two riflemen firing at Japanese located to their front, while behind them three riflemen and one BAR team carefully move northward.

Japanese view: An officer of the 2nd Infantry Regiment is looking southward from his position located along the east side of Hill 200, toward the landing beaches. In the distance he can see Peleliu's airfield and the structures around it. Ahead and to the left is a Japanese-held cave entrance, with a 70mm Type 92 infantry gun crewed by four men. Positioned in the jagged coral to the gun's right are three IJA riflemen who are engaging the advancing Marines with rifle fire. On slightly higher ground farther to the right is a two-man LMG team supported by two riflemen. Closer to the observer, and on his right along the rising slope of Hill 200, is a Type 92 HMG, positioned in coral rocks and firing down the slope of Hill 200 toward the southeast.

Analysis

US EFFECTIVENESS

The Marianas operations validated US amphibious doctrine once again. Room for improvement was identified in many aspects, however, such as better waterproofing of equipment, especially radios, and in training and coordination between assault troops and supporting LVT(A)s. Marine infantry commanders reported that LVT(A) units frequently failed to push inland and keep up with the rifle platoons, with many vehicles stopping on the beach and firing on targets of opportunity. Especially noted by Marines was the superiority of the troop-carrying LVT-4, equipped with a rear ramp, for carrying troops and equipment ashore. In particular, having troops debark through the rear of the LVT-4 via the ramp helped reduce casualties when compared to climbing over the sides of older-model LVTs under fire. The issue remained, however, that many US Navy officers tended to overestimate the effectiveness of pre-invasion naval and air bombardment. This was partially because these officers, familiar with the destruction caused by naval shells striking ships, assumed that the effects of shelling ashore were similar.

At Peleliu the naval-gunfire preparation was unable to destroy or neutralize Japanese defenses as effectively as it had in the past. This partially resulted from Japan's new, and unexpected, doctrine. The Japanese defenses on Peleliu were built in depth and inland of the beach. They utilized the island's caves and manmade tunnels to protect troops and weapons, and extensive camouflage and concealment helped to degrade target location. The result was that both flanks of the landing beaches were enfiladed when the US assault waves landed. This fire inflicted losses that hampered the Marines on the first day's operations. IIIAC reported: "The caves ... presented a problem that so far has not been successfully solved by any supporting arm" (quoted in Hough 1950: 181). The US pre-invasion bombardment did blast away the vegetation covering Peleliu and exposed the rugged terrain of the coral ridges

Marine riflemen operating in the rugged and jungle-covered terrain of the Umurbrogol Ridge attack a Japanese position using hand grenades and Molotov cocktails. The short line-of-sight distances are evident in this photograph. In many cases, Marines were unaware of the existence of a Japanese position until they literally stumbled upon it. (Keystone/Getty Images)

and reduced concealment. Once ashore, naval-gunfire liaison teams with the Marines were able to locate targets and direct pinpoint shelling from ships offshore that was almost always effective.

The most important new weapon used by US forces attacking Peleliu was the long-range flamethrower. These were mounted on LVTs, which were the only vehicles usable in the time available before the assault. The LVT proved a poor choice as a flamethrower mount in combat, however; it was highly vulnerable to enemy fire and, once identified by the Japanese, became a prime target. A flamethrower mount was quickly developed for the M4 medium tank and tank-mounted flamethrowers were used in subsequent US operations. With Japanese defenders now using caves and tunnels as fighting positions, combat-engineer assault detachments assumed greater importance. Demolition teams were in high demand for assaulting cave-tunnel complexes in order to reduce losses to US rifle squads and platoons.

On all three islands, victory depended on the Marine riflemen in the end. Whether landing on a beach, clearing Japanese positions, advancing against defenders in hilly terrain and jungle, or fighting determined enemy combatants in caves and tunnels, US Marine Corps rifle platoons were in contact with the Japanese and suffered the majority of casualties. The Corps' insistence that every Marine was trained as a rifleman proved critically important on Guam and Peleliu. On these islands, artillerymen, engineers, pioneers, service troops, and headquarters personnel picked up their rifles and entered the front lines, defending and attacking as and when needed. Infantry battalions on Peleliu were able to continue their missions for as long as they did only because of extemporized replacements provided by the 1st Marine Division from within its own ranks.

JAPANESE EFFECTIVENESS

After the IJN was defeated at the Battle of the Philippine Sea, the only way to stop the westward advance of US forces across the Pacific was to destroy US amphibious assaults on the beach. On Saipan and Guam, IJA and IJN ground forces intended to do so in accordance with their established doctrine, but this doctrine proved a failure when it met the doctrine, technologies, and tactics of a US amphibious assault.

The first crack in the Marianas' defense was the IJN coastal artillery's inability to engage the US Navy successfully. With the US forces benefiting from dedicated air observation for targeting ships' fires and hundreds of dive-bombing sorties, IJN coastal batteries were either destroyed or neutralized. On D-day, surviving Japanese coastal guns were quickly targeted as soon as they fired and soon neutralized.

Second, IJA artillery on Saipan and Guam did not live up to the expectations of Japanese doctrine developers. Artillery plans captured on Saipan appeared thorough, but their execution was poor. D-day on Saipan saw the Japanese concentrate their shelling on the reefs and beaches. Once the US landing force reached the shoreline, Japanese artillery fire was conducted by batteries, sections, or individual gun crews. Many of the guns were tasked individually to fire on predetermined sight lines and did not aim at particular targets. Other guns were used singly as infantry-support weapons until their positions were overrun. In their artillery plans, 15 percent of Japanese artillery ammunition was allocated for the destruction of approaching landing craft, 15 percent for engaging enemy on the beach, 20 percent for fighting after the landing, and 50 percent was held in reserve.

The deficiencies of Japanese artillery stemmed from the IJA's fundamental failure to appreciate modern mechanized warfare, with artillery viewed as an infantry-support weapon. Compared to other major armies of the 1940s, the IJA was poorly served by its artillery. The structure of the ocean divisions fielded in the Central Pacific highlighted this defect; no divisional artillery headquarters was provided, and artillery was parceled out to infantry regiments and placed under the regiments' control. Additionally, no senior Japanese artillery headquarters, such as an artillery brigade, was deployed on the islands to provide overarching control of artillery and to mass and coordinate fires.

The third Japanese failure was insufficient infantry strength to defend the beaches of Saipan and Guam adequately. For example, on Saipan the 4th, 5th, 6th (less one platoon), and 8th (less one platoon) Rifle companies with the 2d Infantry Gun Company of the IJA's 136th Infantry Regiment were deployed along 4,500yd of shoreline where the 2d Marine Division landed on June 15. Against these, the 2d Marine Division landed four reinforced infantry battalions abreast, which were led by a full battalion of 75mm howitzer-armed LVT(A)-4s. Two more infantry battalions were landed as regimental reserves. The Japanese deployed infantry similarly on all the landing beaches on Saipan and Guam. With their troops positioned on and immediately behind the beaches, the Japanese were subjected to the massive firepower of the US Navy. Although the defenders inflicted significant casualties, they were overwhelmed by fires from naval guns, LVT(A)s, tanks, and Marine riflemen.

Fourth, Japanese counterattacks sacrificed strength in the early days of the Saipan and Guam battles for no gain. Attacks by small forces provided lucrative targets to individual Marines and naval gunfire. Japanese tanks proved vulnerable

Japanese soldiers killed during the battle for Guam, July 1944. The IJA's doctrinal devotion to the offensive led to heavy casualties and few, if any, gains against the Americans in the Pacific. The 29th Division's attack against the 3d Marine Division destroyed the IJA infantry's leadership and inflicted heavy casualties among the attackers, thereby aiding the US efforts by reducing Japanese resistance during the remainder of the campaign. (© CORBIS/Corbis via Getty Images)

to US antitank weapons and armor-piercing .50-caliber machine-gun rounds, and were unsuited to engaging US tanks in combat. On Guam, the Japanese counterattack on the night of July 25/26 was acknowledged by Marines as having been well planned and coordinated. Unfortunately for the Japanese, heavy losses during the preceding days had taken a heavy toll of trained infantry and they were forced to fill out their ranks with service and support personnel. Many of these troops lacked infantry field skills and quickly became casualties during the attack. Loss of infantry officers and senior enlisted leaders early in both battles left the IJA on Saipan and Guam without a cadre to lead even improvised defenders effectively. Many times, defending Japanese chose to launch suicidal charges rather than fight on from caves and natural defenses to prolong the battle.

After Saipan and Guam the Japanese high command recognized the futility of their doctrine of attempting to annihilate a landing on the beach. Operations in the Gilberts, Marshals, and Marianas had demonstrated the US ability to employ devastating pre-invasion naval and air bombardments to overcome well-fortified beach defenses. In response, Imperial General Headquarters issued new orders governing island defense in July 1944. Units were directed to prepare main lines of resistance inland from beaches that minimized the effects of the pre-invasion bombardments. Defenses were now organized in depth and designed to wear down the US forces while amassing sufficient reserves to mount successful counterattacks at appropriate times. After the war, General Clifton B. Cates, the 19th Commandant of the US Marine Corps, described the effects of this new doctrine:

At Peleliu the enemy proved that he had profited from his bitter experiences of earlier operations. He applied intelligently the lessons we had taught him in the Solomons, Gilberts, Marshalls, and Marianas. At Peleliu the enemy made no suicidal banzai charges to hasten the decision; he carefully concealed his plans and dispositions. He nursed from his inferior strength the last ounce of resistance and delay, to extract the maximum cost from his conquerors. In these respects Peleliu differed significantly from previous campaigns and set the pattern for things to come: Iwo Jima and Okinawa. (Quoted in Hough 1950: iii)

Aftermath

The IJN's defeat at the Battle of the Philippine Sea, followed by the loss of Saipan, caused the fall of Japan's Prime Minister General Tojo Hideki and his government. On July 18, the Prime Minister and his entire cabinet submitted their resignations, effective July 22. After these resignations, the IJN and IJA jointly issued a public report on the battle for Saipan that, surprisingly, provided an accurate account of their defeat. This was the first time that the Japanese public had been given a truthful account of negative war news. This was followed within weeks by announcements that Tinian and Guam in the Marianas had been captured by US forces. Japan's Home Islands were now threatened as Tokyo and other major cities were within range of USAAF B-29 long-range heavy bombers flying from bases on Saipan, Tinian, and Guam.

As fighting continued on Peleliu over a month after the 1st Marine Division's assault, US forces under General Douglas MacArthur, supported by the US Pacific Fleet, landed on Leyte Island in the Central Philippines on October 20, 1944. Within days the US Third and Seventh fleets decisively defeated the IJN's Combined Fleet in the battle of Leyte Gulf. The Allied front line in the Pacific had moved over 3,400nmi west in the 11 months since the 2d Marine Division assaulted Tarawa Atoll in the Gilberts on November 20, 1943. These 11 months of war had shown that the IJN could not defeat the US Navy, and that the IJA and IJN land forces could not prevent US forces from capturing islands through amphibious assaults.

With the capture of Peleliu, approximately 25,000 IJA and IJN personnel were stranded on the rest of the Palaus and effectively out of the war. In total, the 11-month advance across the Central Pacific left roughly 125,000 IJA and IJN personnel isolated on islands bypassed in the Central Pacific; islands such Wake, Marcus, Ponape, Ocean, Nauru, Truk, and many others. Once the seas were controlled by the US Navy and a few selected islands captured, these fortified islands had no strategic value. For their garrisons, life became a struggle for survival, growing or foraging for food to avoid

Portrait of a weary Marine on Peleliu. The intensity of combat, the strain of moving through, up, and down, coral ridges covered with jungle, the possibility of ambush, ever-increasing casualties, and a lack of sleep wore out Marines both physically and mentally. The 1st Marines had lost most of its front-line riflemen after a few days of combat on the beach and the Umurbrogol Ridge. On D+6, the regiment was pulled out of the line and soon left the island to recover at its base in the Solomon Islands. (© CORBIS/Corbis via Getty Images)

starvation, enduring US air attacks, and on occasion shelling passing ships.

Japanese forces on Saipan, Guam, and Peleliu had been effectively destroyed and their units removed from the Imperial order of battle. Such were the fates of the 31st Army, 43d Division, 29th Division, 14th Division, 47th IMB, 48th IMB, and 10th IMR. The last three units were formed from detachments making up about one-third each of the veteran 1st, 11th, and 25th divisions, which weakened these formations in further combat, as happened to the 1st Division, which was sent into battle on Leyte against the US Army. The Japanese began to garrison and fortify the Ryukyu and Ogasawara (Bonin) islands, which constituted their last line of defense before the Home Islands. The new defense doctrine that sought to prolong resistance and inflict maximum casualties on US forces that Marines encountered on Peleliu became the foundation for the defensive plans and operations of Japanese garrisons on Okinawa and Iwo Jima in these island groups.

Despite heavy casualties, Marine units were restored to strength and went on to new battles. VAC began planning and preparing for the capture of Iwo Jima, in the Bonins, soon after Tinian was secured. After commanding the Peleliu operation its sister corps, IIIAC, came under the command of the Tenth US Army and started preparations for assaulting Okinawa, in the Ryukyus, alongside the US Army's XXIV Corps.

After Peleliu, the 1st Marine Division moved to Pavuvu Island, in the Solomons, to prepare for another battle. This came on April 1, 1945, when, as part of IIIAC, Tenth US Army, the division assaulted Okinawa and entered an 82-day battle for that island. Having experienced Japan's new defense-in-depth doctrine and use of caves on Peleliu, the 1st Marine Division found many similarities in the Okinawa battle.

After being rebuilt on Saipan, the 2d Marine Division participated in the capture of Okinawa as part of IIIAC and Tenth US Army. The division was initially the army floating reserve and held out of combat. Only one of its infantry regiments, the 8th Marines, was used ashore.

Refitted on Guam, the 3d Marine Division was assigned to VAC for the invasion of Iwo Jima. As part of VAC it served as the corps' floating reserve and did not land in the assault waves on February 19. The division, less the 3d Marines which was kept afloat, landed on Iwo Jima during February 21–24 and fought on the island.

The 4th Marine Division returned to Hawaii before also fighting on Iwo Jima as part of VAC, being one of the two assault divisions on February 19, the other being the new 5th Marine Division. The 1st Provisional Marine

Assault on Leyte Island in the Central Philippines, October 20, 1944. This is a view of the Northern landing area, as landing craft head for the beach. Fighting was still raging on Peleliu as the combined forces of General Douglas MacArthur's Southwest Pacific Area and Admiral Chester W. Nimitz's Pacific Ocean Area began the liberation of the Philippines. In 11 months, American forces had advanced over 3,300nmi from Tarawa Atoll to Leyte. The amphibious assaults on Saipan, Guam, Peleliu, Eniwetok Atoll, Kwajalein, Makin, and Tarawa Atoll had built the path to liberate the Philippines and defeat Japan. (USN 80-G-286843)

Brigade went to Guadalcanal and was expanded into the 6th Marine Division, which fought on Okinawa under IIIAC.

As the war in the Pacific passed the third anniversary of the Japanese attack on Pearl Harbor, the Empire of Japan was facing defeat. The only rational hope Japan had of avoiding total defeat was to inflict as many losses upon the Allies as possible such that they would be compelled to negotiate a peace. The United States and United Kingdom had, however, issued their demand for unconditional surrender at the Casablanca Conference on January 24, 1943. Several more months of war lay ahead for the Pacific.

One of the driving reasons for the Marianas operation was to provide bases for the new B-29 Superfortress heavy bomber. On November 24, 1944, this B-29, "Dauntless Dotty," led 110 other B-29s on the first bombing raid on Tokyo conducted from Saipan. The raiders were the 73d Bombardment Wing USAAF, led by their wing commander, Brigadier General Emmett O'Donnell, Jr. Two years, 11 months and 17 days had passed since the devastating Japanese attack on Pearl Harbor. (Keystone/Getty Images)

UNIT ORGANIZATIONS

US Marine Corps

The Series F infantry battalion included a battalion headquarters and headquarters company (261 all ranks) and three rifle companies (247 each). The headquarters company contained the battalion's mortar platoon (58 men with four 81mm mortars). The battalion also had 18 .30-caliber M1917A1 water-cooled HMGs that could be, and frequently were, used to replace the rifle companies' air-cooled LMGs.

The rifle companies were designated within a regiment by letters: A, B, and C for the 1st Battalion; E, F, and G for the 2d Battalion; and I, K, and L for the 3d Battalion. Each rifle company consisted of a 53-man headquarters (including a 20-man mortar section with three 60mm M2 mortars), one 56-man machine-gun platoon with six .30-caliber M1919A4 air-cooled LMGs, and three rifle platoons (46 each). The company headquarters also had three 2.36in M1A1 "Bazooka" rocket launchers. The rifle platoon had a seven-man headquarters and three 13-man rifle squads. Each squad had one squad leader and three four-man fire-teams that included an M1918A2 Browning Automatic Rifle.

Series F infantry regiments supported their battalions with a 208-man regimental weapons company. Each of these companies had four combat platoons, three with four 37mm M3A1 towed antitank guns (and two "Bazooka" rocket launchers) and a single platoon with four 75mm halftrack-mounted guns known as the M3 SPM (self-propelled mount). The regimental weapons company's headquarters also had 17 "Bazooka" rocket launchers.

Imperial Japanese Army

The ocean division's island-defense regiment had a theoretical strength of 3,165 men in three infantry battalions, one artillery battalion, an engineer company, a supply company, and a medical unit. The regiment was armed with 1,312 Type 99 rifles, 108 Type 89 grenade dischargers, 108 Type 99 LMGs, 18 Type 92 HMGs, six 37mm Type 94 antitank guns, six 70mm infantry howitzers, and 12 75mm field or mountain guns. Each infantry battalion had three rifle companies and one gun company. Each rifle company had 154 men and contained a headquarters (67 all ranks), one machine-gun platoon (two Type 92 HMGs and 20 men), and three rifle platoons. A rifle platoon had a two-man headquarters, four rifle squads (one NCO and six privates) each with one LMG, and one grenadier squad (one NCO and eight privates) with four Type 89 grenade launchers. The gun company had two platoons, one with two 70mm infantry howitzers and the other with two 37mm Type 94 antitank guns.

The ocean division's amphibious regiment had 3,964 men organized into a headquarters company, engineer company, light-tank company, machine-cannon company (20mm automatic guns), and three infantry battalions.

Each infantry battalion had three rifle companies, a mortar company, a battalion artillery company, and an assault pioneer platoon. Each rifle company had 197 men organized into three rifle platoons and one weapons platoon armed with 118 Type 99 rifles, 12 grenade dischargers, 12 LMGs, two HMGs, two 81mm mortars, and one 20mm antitank rifle. The mortar company was authorized 141 men and 12 81mm mortars. The artillery company had 121 men with three 75mm regimental guns and two 37mm antitank guns. The pioneer platoon had 66 men with 63 Type 99 rifles, two flamethrowers, three 81mm mortars, and one 50mm mortar. These battalions did not use the 70mm infantry howitzer issued to most IJA battalions.

On paper, independent infantry battalions on Saipan, Guam, and Peleliu contained a headquarters (75 all ranks), three rifle companies (115 each), one machine-gun company (123), one infantry-gun company (87), and one pioneer platoon (67). Authorized weapons included 318 rifles, 27 LMGs, 12 HMGs, 27 grenade launchers, two 70mm Type 92 infantry howitzers, and two 37mm antitank guns. The infantry battalions of the 9th and 10th IMRs were similarly organized.

BIBLIOGRAPHY

Primary sources

1st Battalion 1st Marines. *Historical Report, Peleliu.* November 23, 1944.

2d Battalion 1st Marines. *Historical Report, Peleliu.* No date.

3d Battalion 1st Marines. *Peleliu Operation Record of Events 26 August 1944 to 10 October 1944.* No date.

3d Marine Division. *Special Action Report.* August 19, 1944.

III Amphibious Corps. *Report on Marianas Islands – Guam, Volumes 1, 2, and 3.* September 3, 1944.

4th Marine Division. *Operations Report, Saipan 15 June to 9 July 1944.* September 18, 1944.

4th Tank Battalion. *Combat Report, Saipan.* August 20, 1944.

23d Marines. *Special Action Report, Saipan.* September 3, 1944.

Co. B, 4th Tank Battalion. *Combat Report.* August 25, 1944.

Co. C, 4th Tank Battalion. *Combat Report.* August 20, 1944.

Commander Joint Expeditionary Force (Commander Amphibious Forces US Pacific Fleet). *Report of Amphibious Operations for the capture of the Marianas Islands (FORAGER Operation).* August 25, 1944.

Engineer, Expeditionary Troops (Task Force 56). *Report on Japanese Defensive Plan for the Island of Saipan Southern Marianas.* July 1944.

First Demobilization Bureau (1946a). *Central Pacific Operations Record, Volume 1.* Japanese Monograph 48. Military History Section, Japanese Research Division, Headquarters, Army Forces Far East.

First Demobilization Bureau (1946b). *Central Pacific Operations Record, Volume 2: The Palau Operation.* Japanese Monograph 49. Military History Section, Japanese Research Division, Headquarters, Army Forces Far East. September 1946.

Garand, George W. & Truman R. Strobridge (1971). *Western Pacific Operations: History of U.S. Marine Corps Operations in World War II, Vol. III.* Historical Branch, G-3 Division, Headquarters, US Marine Corps.

Headquarters Expeditionary Troops, Task Force 56. *G2 Report, Forager Operation.* August 31, 1944.

Headquarters Expeditionary Troops, Task Force 56. *Report by G3 on Forager.* September 4, 1944.

Hoffman, Major Carl W. USMC (1950). *Saipan.* Historical Division Headquarters, US Marine Corps.

Hough, Major Frank O. USMCR (1950). *The Assault on Peleliu.* Historical Division Headquarters, US Marine Corps.

Lodge, Major O.R. USMC (1954). *The Recapture of Guam.* Historical Division Headquarters, US Marine Corps.

MID (1945). *Japanese Defense Against Amphibious Operations.* Special Series No. 29. Washington, DC: Military Intelligence Division, US War Department.

MILS (1945). *Saipan Garrison Plan for 1st Expeditionary Force.* Fort Snelling, MN: Military Intelligence Language School. February 10, 1945.

Shaw, H.I., Jr., B.C. Nalty, & E.T. Turnbladh (1966). *Central Pacific Drive: History of U. S. Marine Corps Operations in World War II, Vol. III.* Historical Branch, G-3 Division, Headquarters, US Marine Corps.

TM-E-30-480 (1944). *Handbook on Japanese Military Forces.* War Department Technical Manual TME-30-480. October 1, 1944. Available at https://www.ibiblio.org/hyperwar/Japan/IJA/HB/

TP-167 (1938). *Landing Operations Doctrine: United States Navy.* Office of the Chief of Naval Operations, Division of Training. Available at https://archive.org/details/landingoperation00unit_0

Secondary sources

Crowl, Philip A. (1993). *Campaign in the Marianas.* Washington, DC: US Government Printing Office.

Hunt, George P. (1946). *Coral Comes High.* New York, NY: Harper & Bros.

Moran, Jim & G.L. Rottman (2002). *Peleliu 1944.* Campaign 110. Oxford: Osprey Publishing.

Morison, Samuel Eliot (1953). *History of United States Naval Operations in World War II: New Guinea and the Marianas, March 1944–August 1944.* Boston, MA: Little Brown & Co.

Ness, Leland (2015). *Rikugun: Guide to Japanese Ground Forces 1937-1945: Volume 1 – Tactical Organization of Imperial Japanese Army & Navy Ground Forces.* Warwick: Helion & Co.

Rottman, G.L. (2004a). *Guam 1941 & 1944.* Campaign 139. Oxford: Osprey Publishing.

Rottman, G.L. (2004b). *Saipan & Tinian 1944.* Campaign 137. Oxford: Osprey Publishing.

Rottman, G.L. (2004c). US Marine *Corps Pacific Theater of Operations 1943–44.* Battle Orders 7. Oxford: Osprey Publishing.

Rottman, G.L. (2004d). *US Marine Corps Pacific Theater of Operations 1944–45.* Battle Orders 8. Oxford: Osprey Publishing.

INDEX

References to illustrations are shown in **bold**.
References to plates are shown in bold with
caption pages in brackets, e.g. **40–41**, (42).